شرح

الأرجوزة الميئية في ذكرحال أشرف البرية

An Explanation of One Hundred Lines of Poetry in Memory of the Noblest of Creation

Ibn Abi'l Ezz Al Hanafi

Explained by

Abdul Razaq Bin Abdul Muhsin Al Badr

Translated by

Sami AK Noor

AuthorHouse™
1663 Liberty Drive
Bloomington, IN 47403
www.authorhouse.com
Phone: 1 (800) 839-8640

Published by AuthorHouse 04/24/2017

ISBN: 978-1-5049-8170-5 (sc)
ISBN: 978-1-5049-8171-2 (hc)
ISBN: 978-1-5049-8172-9 (e)

Library of Congress Control Number: 2016910153

Print information available on the last page.

Translators Note:

The translation of the text of the poem has not been converted exactly word for word in an attempt to rhyme the English couplets together for ease and memorization purposes. This explanation written by Ash Shaykh Abdul Razaq has been translated also as a further elobarartion of Al Hanafee's classical masterpiece.

The Arabic couplets have been kept to maintain the authenticity of the poetry and to clarify the meanings of some of the purposeful Arabic vocabulary mentioned by the Author. The reader must bare in mind that this work is an abridged version of the Prophet's Seerah and has not delved into great detail regarding some events. It is an effort which is contrary to other biographies that you may find and acts as a reference more than anything else. It is a translation that can be used for memorization, reference, citing and to compare the opinions and views of the scholars of Al Islam regarding the life and times of the Messenger of Allah ﷺ.

I felt the need to translate this work as there is a lack of engaging methods to learn the biography of the Prophet Muhammad ﷺ by way of reading. The non Arab readers are at a disadvantage due to the limited access of Islamic poetry that is widely available in the Islamic books written in Arabic. This work will serve the students of knowledge and young people to study the life of the greatest man that ever lived Muhammad ibn Abdullah ﷺ. It refers back to the people of knowledge and earlier generations of the Sunnah. My primary objective in this simple effort is to facilitate the reader to become closer to the Messenger of Allah ﷺ through love, obedience, reverence and emulation.

I would like to highly stress the portions of this book pertaining to conflict, battle and warfare need to be understood in the correct context of his biography. Some additional footnotes have been added in order to assist the reader of not misunderstanding or misinterpreting the text.

Permission of this work has been authorized by Sh. Abdul Razzaq Bin Badr who has stated he has no legal rights to the book. Additionally, this work has been checked and approved of by Dr. Aladdin Ahmed who is a professor and lecturer at the King Abdul Aziz University in Jeddah, Kingdom of Saudi Arabia.

May Allah (The Most High and Majestic) forgive me for any mistakes I may have made in the translation of this work (as I will be fully responsible) and guide us all to His obedience to loving His Prophet ﷺ. Finally, as a gesture and a token of goodwill I request the reader to make dua (supplication) for me and my family for goodness in this life and the hereafter.

Sami Abdul Kahir Noor

In the Name of Allah

Introduction to the Explanation

All praises due to Allah the Lord of the worlds, I testify that Allah is one who has no partners and I testify that Muhammad is His servant and Messenger ﷺ and may the peace be upon his companions.

Indeed, nothing is hidden from the believer when he studies the biography of the Prophet ﷺ from its blessed legacy, many benefits and lessons for the believer to accumulate in this world and the hereafter.

His life and times ﷺ is the most beautiful biography which can purify the inner thoughts and feelings of the servants. This is the life of the most pious imam (leader) and the best example for the whole of mankind; he is the master of the children of Adam (Upon him is peace).

In studying this biography, we find the description which Allah (The Most High) sent as an example for His servants when he revealed:

﴿لَقَدْ كَانَ لَكُمْ فِي رَسُولِ اللَّهِ أُسْوَةٌ حَسَنَةٌ لِمَنْ كَانَ يَرْجُو اللَّهَ وَالْيَوْمَ الْآخِرَ وَذَكَرَ اللَّهَ كَثِيرًا﴾

{There has certainly been for you in the Messenger of Allah an excellent example for anyone whose hope is in Allah and the Last Day and [who] remembers Allah often} (Al Ahzaab: 21)

This deepens the love and reserves a place in your heart for him ﷺ as the Messenger of Allah himself stated:

"None of you truly believe until I am more beloved to him than his parents, his children and the whole of mankind".[1]

This is a great path for the servant to follow and emulate the Prophet of Allah ﷺ in real life. We find that certain aspects of his life enthuse a person to be guided and to know with truth who the Messenger of Allah really ﷺ is.

The classical scholars from the people of knowledge along with the contemporaries have published poetised versions of the prophet's biography so it may easily spread. These writings have been beneficial and their authors are well-known.

Some of these writings were deliberately made brief in order to be distributed in mass volume. All these efforts act as an introduction and an opening for the new beginner to embody and pass on this blessed knowledge. Before us is a beneficial poem and a good treatise on our beloved Prophet ﷺ. This is a shortened version of the path of the Prophet depicting the journey he embarked upon written with great precision and simplicity. Therein are a hundred couplets which are easy for many to understand in reference to the great events and occurences from the life of Allah's Apostle, Muhammad ﷺ. Its lessons are beautiful, its wording is simple and stories are unmistakeably clear.

I recited this poem to my father (May Allah preserve him) which he was pleased with and we benefitted from its knowledge a great deal. He was astonished of how inviting and fluent the style was with its magnificent narrative and held to be exceptionally poetic. He (May Allah preserve him) then said to me "This poem is beautiful and easy to comprehend, the stories are authentically established and validated by other biographies alongside his available citations". We also know its name as

[1] Sahih Bukharee no.15, Muslim no.44 Hadith of Anas ibn Malik

'*A Hundred Lines of Poetry*' which was mentioned by the writer (May Allah have mercy on him) in the conclusion of this poem.

He finished by calling it ***'A Hundred Lines of Poetry in Memory of the Noblest of Creation'***.

The author had studied with great teachers from the people of the Sunnah. He was an Imam himself from the people of knowledge and is well-known for his established writings and beneficial publications, not to forget his famous work '*The Commentary of Al Aqeedah at-Tahaweeyah*' which is a tremendous book with many benefits therein.[2]

Ali Bin Ali Bin Muhammad Bin Abi'l Izz Al Dimashqi Al Hanafee who passed away in the year 792 Hijri was an Imam and a Judge[3].

He started to learn religion and its virtues while he was still very young. He was brought up with knowledge and had a love for the scholars and listening to them. He had benefited greatly from his teachers who were the spectacular leaders and researchers of their time.

From them were the likes of Imam ibn Kathir (May Allah have mercy on him), a man of marvellous treatise and books; an excellent researcher of biographies and history from whom he learned immensely.

Ibn Abi Al Ezz had also referenced his own books such as '*The Commentary of Aqeedah Tahaweeyah*' and records in the citings 'Our

---

[2] I benefitted greatly from this book at the beginning of my studies and we continued with this book in our second and third year of our journey in the university. I am still extracting much benefit from this book from time to time. I also haven't cut off my revision with it. (By) Publishing this work is my way of showing great loyalty to the Shaykh, we ask Allah to give him the highest level in (the) Paradise

[3] Also see the biography called 'Abnaa il Ghumr Bi'Abnaa Il Umr' (409/1) and Durar Al Kaminah' (87/3) by Ibn Hajr. Also 'Shathraat Al Dhahab' by Ibn Imad Al Hanbalee (557/8). His name is also mentioned as Muhammad ibn Alee by others but this is incorrect.

shaykh, Shaykh Imad Ad-Deen Ibn Kathir'[1]. The author remained with the latter and absorbed his knowledge like a sponge then he went on to compose this poem so it appears to be a summary of the work of his teacher Ibn Kathir's detailed *Seerah.* We also observe this in his speech in the opening lines of the poem.

وَبَعْدُ هَاكَ سِيرَةَ الرَّسُولِ مَنْظُومَةً مُوجَزَةَ الْفُصُولِ

Here's the life of the Mesenger of our Lord

in precise divided chapters that we'll explore

It is well known that his Shaykh ibn Katheer has written an explanatory work called '*Al Fusool fee Seeratil Rasool*' ﷺ.

Shaykh Abdul Razzaq Bin Abdul Muhsin Al Badr

[1] Pages (703, 460, 277) in 'Sharh Aqeedatil Wasitiyah fi Aqeedah Salafiyyah' revised edition by Dr. Abdullah Turki & Shuayb Al Arna'oot.

The Classical Poem; Al Arjoozatu'l Mi'eeyah Fi Thikri Haal Ashraf il Bareeyah

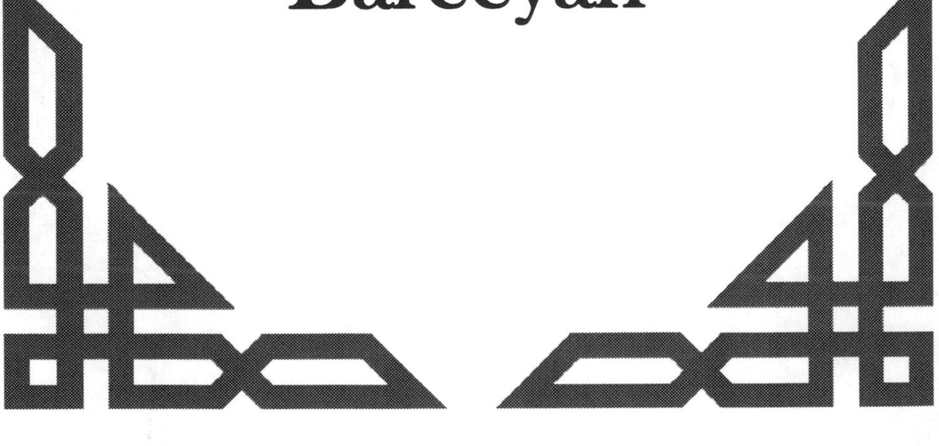

اَلْحَمْدُ للهِ الْقَدِيمِ الْبَارِي ثُمَّ صَلاَتُهُ عَلَى الْمُخْتَارِ

All praise to Allah, the Pre–Eternal One who designs

then prayers upon His chosen of mankind.

وَبَعْدُ هَاكَ سِيرَةَ الرَّسُولِ مَنْظُومَةً مُوجَزَةَ الْفُصُولِ

Here's the life of the Messenger of our Lord

in precise divided chapters that we'll explore.

وُلِد فِي عَاشِرِ الْفَضِيلِ رَبِيعِ الأَوَّلِ عَامَ الْفِيلِ

Born in the days of the virtuous ten

Rabee al Awwal, the year elephant

لَكِنَّمَا الْمَشْهُورُ ثَانِي عَشْرِهِ فِي يَوْمِ الاِثْنَيْنِ طُلُوعَ فَجْرِه

The twelth day, by far the most famous

Monday's rising of dawn amazingly gracious

وَوَافَقَ الْعِشْرِينَ مِنْ نَيْسَانَا وَقَبْلَه حَيْنُ أَبِيهِ حَانَا

Corresponding to April on the 20th day

before this event his father passed away

وَبَعْدَ عَامَيْنِ غَدَا فَطِيمَا   جَاءَتْ بِهِ مُرضِعُهُ سَلِيمَا

Two years later of initial weaning

she returned with him in a condition that was pleasing

حَلِيمَةٌ لِأُمِّهِ وَعَادَتْ   بِهِ لِأَهْلِهَا كَمَا أَرَادَتْ

Halimah, to his mother and with him returned

back to her family as desired and yearned

فَبَعْدَ شَهْرَيْنِ انْشِقَاقُ بَطْنِهِ   وَقِيلَ بَعْدَ أَرْبَعٍ مِنْ سِنِّهِ

Two months later his chest was split

around four years old and a bit.

وَبَعْدَ سِتٍّ مَعَ شَهْرٍ جَاءِ   وَفَاةُ أُمِّهِ عَلَى الْأَبْوَاءِ

After six years and a month he faced

the passing of his mother in Abwaa'aa place

وَجَدُّه لِلْأَبِ عَبْدُ الْمُطَّلِبْ   بَعْدَ ثَمَانٍ مَاتَ مِنْ غَيْرِ كَذِبْ

His grandfather Abdul Mutallib died on this date

no rumour it was when the Prophet was eight

ثُمَّ أَبُو طَالِبٍ الْعَمُّ كَفَلْ خِدْمَتَهُ ثُمَّ إِلَى الشَّامِ رَحَلْ

Then with Abu Taalib, his uncle of protection

he proceeded on a trip in the Shaam direction

وَذَاكَ بَعْدَ عَامِهِ الثَّانِي عَشَرْ وَكَانَ مِنْ أَمْرِ (بَحِيرَا) مَا اشْتَهَرْ

Then that year was the twelfth of his age

something occured, that to amaze

وَسَارَ نَحْوَ الشَّامِ أَشْرَفُ الْوَرَى فِي عَامِ خَمْسَةٍ وَعِشْرِينَ اذْكُرَا

Again to sham the noblest of all

in his twenty fifth year this event we recall

لِأُمِّنَا خَدِيجَةٍ مُتَّجِرَا وَعَادَ فِيهِ رَابِحًا مُسْتَبْشِرَا

For our mother Khadijah he did trade

returned again happy with a profit made

فَكَانَ فِيهِ عَقْدُهُ عَلَيْهَا وَبَعْدَهُ إِفْضَاؤُهُ إِلَيْهَا

Then the contract with her was dated

next the marriage consummated

وَوِلْدُهُ مِنْهَا خَلاَ إِبْرَاهِيمْ فَالأَوَّلُ الْقَاسِمُ حَازَ التَّكْرِيمْ

Except Ibraheem his children she bore

the first was Al Qasim honored and more

وَزَيْنَبٌ رُقَيَّةٌ وَفَاطِمَةْ وَأُمُّ كُلْثُومٍ لَهُنَّ خَاتِمَةْ

Zaynab, Ruqaiyah and Fatimah too

then Umm Kulthoom was the last of the few.

وَالطَّاهِرُ الطَّيِّبُ عَبْدُاللهِ وَقِيلَ كُلٌّ اسْمٍ لِفَرْدٍ زَاهِي

Then Abdullah, the pure and right

their names shining brightly like a single light

وَالْكُلُّ فِي حَيَاتِهِ ذَاقُوا الْحِمَامْ وَبَعْدَهُ فَاطِمَةٌ بِنِصْفِ عَامْ

All in his life their souls did depart

after his was Fatimah with six months apart

وَبَعْدَ خَمْسٍ وَثَلاَثِينَ حَضَرْ بُنْيَانَ بَيْتِ اللهِ لَمَّا أَنْ دَثَرْ

At thirty-five years, he was there with the others

building Allah's house until it was covered

وَحَكَّمُوهُ وَرَضُوا بِمَا حَكَمْ   فِي وَضْعِ ذَاكَ الْحَجَرِ الْأَسْوَدِ ثَمّْ

Pleased and glad with the judgement they faced

placing the black stone in its rightful place

وَبَعْدَ عَامِ أَرْبَعِينَ أُرْسِلاَ   فِي يَوْمِ الاِثْنَيْنِ يَقِينًا فَانْقُلاَ

At 40 years he was inspired with truth

on Monday with revelation as evident proof

فِي رَمَضَانَ أَوْ رَبِيعِ الْأَوَّلِ   وَسُورَةُ اقْرَأْ أَوَّلُ الْمُنَزَّلِ

Rabee Al Awwal or Ramadan

the Chapter 'Read' was revealed from Quran

ثُمَّ الْوُضُوءَ وَالصَّلَاةَ عَلَّمَهْ   جِبْرِيلُ وَهْيَ رَكْعَتَانِ مُحْكَمَةْ

Ablution and prayer was what he was taught

by the mighty Jibreel two rakah sought.

ثُمَّ مَضَتْ عِشْرُونَ يَوْمًا كَامِلَةْ   فَرَمَتِ الْجِنَّ نُجُومٌ هَائِلَ

Next the elapse twenty days

Shooting stars as Jinn left them afraid

ثُمَّ دَعَا فِي أَرْبَعِ الْأَعْوَامِ بِالْأَمْرِ جَهْرَةً إِلَى الْإِسْلَامِ

In the fourth year he did preach

an open call to Islam was his speech

وَأَرْبَعٌ مِنَ النِّسَا وَاثْنَا عَشَرْ مِنَ الرِّجَالِ الصَّحْبِ كُلٌّ قَدْ هَجَرْ

Four of the women left their state

with twelve male companions they did migrate

إِلَى بِلَادِ الْحُبْشِ فِي خَامِسِ عَامْ وَفِيهِ عَادُوا ثُمَّ عَادُوا لَا مَلَامْ

To Abysinnia in the year five

then returned once again a second time

ثَلَاثَةٌ هُمْ وَثَمَانُونَ رَجُلْ وَمَعَهُمْ جَمَاعَةٌ حَتَّى كَمُلْ

Eighty-three from amongst the men

with a group of people they then went.

وَهُنَّ عَشْرٌ وَثَمَانٍ ثُمَّ قَدْ أَسْلَمَ فِي السَّادِسِ حَمْزَةُ الْأَسَدْ

With eighteen women this travel they faced

in the sixth year of Islam, Hamzah embraced

وَبَعْدَ تِسْعٍ مِنْ سِنِي رِسَالَتِهْ　　مَاتَ أَبُو طَالِبَ ذُو كَفَالَتِهْ

After nine years since revelation

Abu Talib died a guard from his nation

وَبَعْدَه خَدِيجَةٌ تُوُفِّيَتْ　　مِنْ بَعْدِ أَيَّامٍ ثَلاَثَةٍ مَضَتْ

Then Khadijah passed away

after his uncle by three days

وَبَعْدَ خَمْسِينَ وَرُبْعٍ أَسْلَمَا　　جِنُّ نَصِيبِينَ وعَادُوا فَاعْلَمَا

After fifty and a quarter the Jinn accepted

returned to teach them they left affected

ثُمَّ عَلَى سَوْدَةَ أَمْضَى عَقْدَهْ　　فِي رَمَضَانَ ثُمَّ كَانَ بَعْدَهْ

Then with Sawdah a contract spent

In Ramadan this was meant

عَقْدُ ابْنَةِ الصِّدِّيقِ فِي شَوَّالِ،　　وَبَعْدَ خَمْسِينَ وَعَامٍ تَالِ

Married Al Sideeq's daughter in the Shawwal days

at over fifty years of age

أُسْرِيْ بِهِ وَالصَّلَوَاتُ فُرِضَتْ   خَمْسًا بِخَمْسِينَ كَمَا قَدْ حُفِظَتْ

Ascended to where the prayer was obliged

then it was known as fifty- five

وَالْبَيْعَةُ الْأُولَى مَعَ اثْنَيْ عَشَرَا   مِنْ أَهْلِ طَيْبَةَ كَمَا قَدْ ذُكِرَا

Twelve took the pledge willing and not ordered

from the city of Taybah as recorded

وَبَعْدَ ثِنْتَيْنِ وَخَمْسِينَ أَتَى   سَبْعُونَ فِي الْمَوْسِمِ هَذَا ثَبَتَا

In his fifty second year they came for a reason

seventy men in this blessed season

مِنْ طَيْبَةٍ فَبَايَعُوا ثُمَّ هَجَرْ   مَكَّةَ يَوْمَ اثْنَيْنِ مِنْ شَهْرِ صَفَرْ

Another pledge from Taybah then he migrated

Makkah on a Monday, Safar dated

فَجَاءَ طَيْبَةَ الرِّضَا يَقِينَا   إِذْ كَمَّلَ الثَّلَاثَ وَالْخَمْسِينَا

Alas he arrived, the land full of pleasure indeed

at the year of his age, fifty-three

فِي يَوْمِ الاِثْنَيْنِ وَدَامَ فِيهَا عَشْرَ سِنِينَ كَمَلَتْ نَحْكِيهَا

There on a Monday he settled to live

for ten whole years, this story we'll give

أَكْمَلَ فِي الْأُولَى صَلَاةَ الْحَضَرِ مِنْ بَعْدِ مَا جَمَّعَ فَاسْمَعْ خَبَرِي

A resident's prayer in the first year being certain

after they gathered hearing the sermon

ثُمَّ بَنَى الْمَسْجِدَ فِي قُبَاءِ وَمَسْجِدَ الْمَدِينَةِ الْغَرَّاءِ

It was built the mosque of Qubaa

a famous place of worship like no other

ثُمَّ بَنَى مِنْ حَوْلِهِ مَسَاكِنَهْ ثُمَّ أَتَى مِنْ بَعْدُ فِي هَذِي السَّنَةْ

Then he built her place close by

later that year, they then arrived

أَقَلُّ مِنْ نِصْفِ الَّذِينَ سَافَرُوا إِلَى بِلَادِ الْحُبْشِ حِينَ هَاجَرُوا

Fewer than half they travelled by fate

again to Abyssinia they did migrate

وَفِيهِ آخَى أَشْرَفُ الْأَخْيَارِ   بَيْنَ الْمُهَاجِرِينَ وَالْأَنْصَارِ

Paired them he did the noblest by far

between the Muhajireen and the Ansaar

ثُمَّ بَنَى بِابْنَةِ خَيْرِ صَحْبِهِ   وَشَرَعَ الْأَذَانَ فَاقْتَدِي بِهِ

Built her place, his best friend's daughter

then explained the athan times as was ordered

وَغَزْوَةُ الْأَبْوَاءِ بَعْدُ فِي صَفَرْ   هَذَا وَفِي الثَّانِيَةِ الْغَزْوُ اشْتَهَرْ

In Safar, Abwaa'aa shown

the second year hijri, a battle well known

إِلَى بُوَاطَ ثُمَّ بَدْرٍ وَوَجَبْ   تَحَوُّلُ الْقِبْلَةِ فِي نِصْفِ رَجَبْ

To Bawaat then Badr arranged

In the middle of Rajab the qiblah changed

مِنْ بَعْدِ ذَا الْعُشَيْرُ يَا إِخْوَانِي   وَفَرْضُ شَهْرِ الصَّوْمِ فِي شَعْبَانِ

Oh my brothers after ten days passing

in Sha'ban came the order of fasting

وَالْغَزْوَةَ الْكُبْرَى الَّتِي بِبَدْرِ   فِي الصَّوْمِ فِي سَابِعِ عَشْرِ الشَّهْرِ

At the Badr this great battle vast

on the seventeenth day of the Ramadan fast

وَوَجَبَتْ فِيهِ زَكَاةُ الْفِطْرِ   مِنْ بَعْدِ بَدْرٍ بِلَيَالٍ عَشْرِ

Next was Zakah al Fitr as commanded

ten nights after the Badr standard

وَفِي زَكَاةِ الْمَالِ خُلْفٌ فَادْرِ   وَمَاتَتِ ابْنَةُ النَّبِيِّ الْبَرِّ

Zakat Al Maal they differed to agree

then the passing of his child upon piety

رُقَيَّةٌ قَبْلَ رُجُوعِ السَّفْرِ   زَوْجَةُ عُثْمَانَ وعُرْسُ الطُّهْرِ

Ruqaiyah it was before he returned to abide

a pure soul, uthman's beautiful bride

فَاطِمَةٍ عَلَى عَلِيِّ الْقَدْرِ   وَأَسْلَمَ الْعَبَّاسُ بَعْدَ الأَسْرِ

Fatimah to Ali, he was in awe

then Abbas embraced this prisoner of war

وَقَيْنُقَاعُ غَزْوُهُمْ فِي الْإِثْرِ بَعْدَ ضَحَاءِ يَوْمِ عِيدِ النَّحْرِ

The aftermath trailed the Qaynuqa invasion

then the sacrificial Eid celebration

وَغَزْوَةُ السَّوِيقِ ثُمَّ قَرْقَرَةْ وَالْغَزْوُ فِي الثَّالِثَةِ الْمُشْتَهِرَةْ

Saweeq and Qarqara then occurred

well known battles in the year of the third

فِي غَطَفَانَ وَبَنِي سُلَيْمِ وَأُمُّ كُلْثُومَ ابْنَةُ الْكَرِيمِ

At Ghatfaan and the tribe of Saleem

Umm Kulthoom, the blessed child of Al Ameen

زَوَّجَ عُثْمَانَ بِهَا وَخَصَّهْ ثُمَّ تَزَوَّجَ النَّبِيُّ حَفْصَةْ

She married Uthmaan specifically

then the Prophet to Hafsah rightfully

وَزَيْنَبًا ثُمَّ غَزَا إِلَى أُحُدْ فِي شَهْرِ شَوَّالٍ وَحَمْراءِ الْأَسَدْ

Zaynab next then Uhud had

In Shawwal, hamratul Asad

فَالْخَمْرُ حُرِّمَتْ يَقِينًا فَاسْمَعَنْ هَذَا وَفِيهَا وُلِدَ السِّبْطُ الْحَسَنْ

Alcohol was forbidden they certainly heard

then Hassan was born in that very same year

وَكَانَ فِي الرَّابِعَةِ الْغَزْوُ إِلَى بَنِي النَّضِيرِ فِي رَبِيعٍ أَوَّلَا

In the fourth it was the battle to be

with the tribe of Nadheer in first of Rabee

وبَعْدُ مَوْتُ زَيْنَبَ الْمُقَدَّمَةْ وَبَعْدَهُ نِكَاحُ أُمِّ سَلَمَةْ

The death of Zaynab was surely close by

Umm Salamah's nikkah was next in line

وَبِنْتِ جَحْشٍ ثُمَّ بَدْرِ الْمَوْعِدِ وَبَعْدَهَا الْأَحْزَابُ فَاسْمَعْ وَاعْدُدِ

The daughter of Jahsh with Badr's account

and hearing the enemies in their enormous amount

ثُمَّ بَنِي قُرَيْظَةٍ وَفِيهِمَا خُلْفٌ وَفِي ذَاتِ الرِّقَاعِ عُلِمَا

The battle of Quraydha next behind

Dhaat Ar Riqaa they learned in time

كَيْفَ صَلاَةُ الْخَوْفِ وَالْقَصْرُ نُمِي　　　وَآيَةُ الْحِجَابِ وَالتَّيَمُّمِ

The prayer of fear and to shorten right

and the verse of hijab and how to wipe

قِيلَ: وَرَجْمُهُ الْيَهُودِيَّيْنِ　　　وَمَوْلِدُ السِّبْطِ الرِّضَا الْحُسَيْنِ

The Jewish couple were publicly punished

and the birth of Hussain pleasingly flourished

اَلْإِفْكُ فِي غَزْوِ بَنِي الْمُصْطَلِقِ　　　وَكَانَ فِي الْخَامِسَةِ اسْمَعْ وَثِقِ

The incident of Al Ifk and the Mustaliq tribe

listen and trust in the year hijrah five

وَدُومَةُ الْجَنْدَلِ قَبْلَ وَحَصَلْ　　　عَقْدُ ابْنَةِ الْحَارِثِ بَعْدُ وَاتَّصَلْ

In the area of Jandal before it took place

a contract to Harith's daughter was embraced

وَعَقْدُ رَيْحَانَةَ فِي ذِي الْخَامِسَةْ　　　ثُمَّ بَنُو لِحْيَانَ بَدْءُ السَّادِسَةْ

Wedded Rayhanah in the fifth of that year

then battled Banu Lihyan in the sixth to occur

وَبَعْدَه اسْتِسْقَاؤُهُ وَذُو قَرَدْ وَصُدَّ عَنْ عُمْرَتِهِ لَمَّا قَصَدْ

After it rained and the Dhi Qird mission

they were prevented from their umrah vision

وَبَيْعَةُ الرِّضْوَانِ أُولَى وَبَنَى فِيهَا بِرَيْحَانَةَ هَذَا بَيِّنَا

The first pledge they built was pleasing and keen

the news of Rayhanah was inbetween

وَفُرِضَ الْحَجُّ بِخُلْفٍ فَاسْمَعَهْ وَكَانَ فَتْحُ خَيْبَرٍ فِي السَّابِعَةْ

The Hajj was obligated dispite what was heard

the conquest of Khaybar in the seventh year

وَحَظْرُ لَحْمِ الْحُمُرِ الْأَهْلِيَّةْ فِيهَا وَمُتْعَةِ النِّسَا الرَّوِيَّةْ

Domesticated donkey's meat not to be consumed

and temporary marriages were refused

ثُمَّ عَلَى أُمِّ حَبِيبَةَ عَقَدْ وَمَهْرَهَا عَنْهُ النَّجَاشِيُّ نَقَدْ

Then with Umm Habibah he wedded next

with Najashi's help, by the text

وَسُمَّ فِي شَاةٍ بِهَا هَدِيَّةْ ثُمَّ اصْطَفَى صَفِيَّةً صَفِيَّةْ

The poisonous sheep a gift he received

then he chose Safiyyah for her manners and deeds

ثُمَّ أَتَتْ وَمَنْ بَقِي مُهَاجِرَا وَعَقْدُ مَيْمُونَةَ كَانَ الآخِرَا

The rest arrived who migrated alas

and then married Maymunah who was the last

وَقَبْلُ إِسْلاَمُ أَبِي هُرَيْرَةْ وَبَعْدُ عُمْرَةُ الْقَضَا الشَّهِيرَةْ

But before was the Islam of Abu Hurayrah

after was the famous Umrah savior

وَالرُّسْلَ فِي مُحَرَّمِ الْمُحَرَّمِ أَرْسَلَهُمْ إِلَى الْمُلُوكِ فَاعْلَمِ

The messengers next in Muharram brought

Islamic letters to the kings they were taught

وَأُهْدِيَتْ مَارِيَةُ الْقِبْطِيَّةْ فِيهِ وَفِي الثَّامِنَةِ السَّرِيَّةْ

Mariah the Coptic was truly a gift stated

in the eighth year delegated

لِمُؤْتَةٍ سَارَتْ وَفِي الصِّيَامِ قَدْ كَانَ فَتْحُ الْبَلَدِ الْحَرَامِ

Mu'tah begun during the fast

then the conquest of the Haram finally passed

وَبَعْدَهُ قَدْ أَوْرَدُوا مَا كَانَ فِي يَوْمِ حُنَيْنٍ ثُمَّ يَوْمِ الطَّائِفِ

Next it was relayed about the day

prior toTaif it was Hunayn

وَبَعْدُ فِي ذِي الْقَعْدَةِ اعْتِمَارُهْ مِنَ الْجِعِرَّانَةِ وَاسْتِقْرَارُهْ

After Dhil Qi'dah his Umrah he started

Ja'irranah to Makkah the Prophet departed

وَبِنْتُهُ زَيْنَبُ مَاتَتْ ثُمَّا مَوْلِدُ إِبْرَاهِيمَ فِيهَا حَتْمَا

His daughter Zaynab passed after some time

Ibrahim was born after she died

وَوَهَبَتْ نَوْبَتَهَا لِعَائِشَةْ سَوْدَةُ مَا دَامَتْ زَمَانًا عَائِشَةْ

She donated to Aishah a great sacrifice

Sawdah with goodness a wonderful wife

وَعُمِلَ الْمِنْبَرُ غَيْرَ مُخْتَفِ وَحجَّ عَتَّابُ بِأَهْلِ الْمَوْقِفِ

A pulpit was made clear to see

then the Hajj of Attab led the city

ثُمَّ تَبُوكَ قَدْ غزَا فِي التَّاسِعَةْ وَهَدَّ مَسْجِدَ الضِّرَارِ رَافِعَهْ

Tabuk a battle in the ninth taking place

destroying Masjid Al Dhiraar after its raise

وَحَجَّ بِالنَّاسِ أَبُو بَكْرٍ وَثَمّْ تَلا بَرَاءَةً عَلِيٌّ وَحَتَم

Abu Bakr lead on the Hajj occasion

then Ali declared the emancipation

أَنْ لَا يَحُجَّ مُشْرِكٌ بَعْدُ وَلاَ يَطُوفُ عَارٍ ذَا بِأَمْرٍ فُعِلاَ

No pagans will perform Hajj on their standard

or make the Tawaaf other than commanded

وَجَاءَتِ الْوُفُودُ فِيهَا تَتْرَى هَذَا وَمِنْ نِسَاهُ آلَى شَهْرَا

The delegations then came in succession

30 days from his wives to teach them a lesson

ثُمَّ النَّجَاشِيَّ نَعَى وَصَلَّى عَلَيْهِ مِنْ طَيْبَة نَالَ الْفَضْلا

Next passed Najashi they grieved and they prayed

upon this good person the virtue was paid

وَمَاتَ إِبْرَاهِيمُ فِي الْعَامِ الْأَخِيرْ وَالْبَجَلِيْ أَسْلَمَ وَاسْمُهُ جَرِيرْ

In the last year Ibraheem's passing then came

Bajali converted and Jareer was his name

وَحَجَّ حِجَّةَ الْوَدَاعِ قَارِنَا وَوَقَفَ الْجُمْعَةَ فِيهَا آمِنَا

Then performed Hajj, the farewell achieved

they stood on the Friday with convicted belief

وَأُنْزِلَتْ فِي الْيَوْمِ بُشْرَى لَكُمُ اَلْيَوْمَ أَكْمَلْتُ لَكُمْ دِينَكُمُ

The news was revealed on that glorious day

the religion has completed nothing taken away

وَمَوْتُ رَيْحَانَةَ بَعْدَ عَوْدِهْ وَالتِّسْعُ عِشْنَ مُدَّةً مِنْ بَعْدِهْ

Rayhanah died after he returned at last

but the nine remained when he did pass

وَيَوْمَ الاِثْنَيْنِ قَضَى يَقِينَا   إِذْ أَكْمَلَ الثَّلاَثَ وَالسِّتِّينَا

Monday it was the judgment decreed

the completion of his life at sixty-three

وَالدَّفْنُ فِي بَيْتِ ابْنَةِ الصِّدِّيقِ   فِي مَوْضِعِ الْوَفَاةِ عَنْ تَحْقِيقِ

Buried in her house, daughter of one who bore truth

a place not denied was evidently proof

وَمُدَّةُ التَّمْرِيضِ خُمْسَا شَهْرِ   وَقِيلَ بَلْ ثُلْثُ وَخُمْسُ فَادْرِ

Strucken with illness for a fifth of 30 nights

yet some say a third but a fifth is whats right.

وَتَمَّتِ الْأُرْجُوزَةُ الْمِيئِيَّةْ   فِي ذِكْرِ حَالِ أَشْرَفِ الْبَرِيَّةْ

We complete this poem of one hundred lines

on the best of creation that was ever alive

صَلَّى عَلَيْهِ اللهُ رَبِّي وَعَلَى   صِحَابِهِ وآلِهِ وَمَنْ تَلا

Prayers be upon him and also upon

his companions and family that continued on.

An Explanation of One Hundred Lines of Poetry In Memory of the Noblest of Creation

اَلْحَمْدُ للهِ الْقَدِيرِ الْبَارِي   ثُمَّ صَلاَتُهُ عَلَى الْمُخْتَارِ

All praise to Allah, The Pre–Eternal One who designs

then prayers upon His chosen of mankind.

The author [May Allah have Mercy on him] begins with the grace and gratitude of Allah [The Most High] and sends a welcome and prayer upon the chosen Messenger of Allah, Muhammad ﷺ.

اَلْحَمْدُ - The gratitude to Allah [The Most High] which is mentioned is out of love and glorification to Him. He [The Most High] should be praised with his most beautiful, highest of names and attributes that should be revered due to the great blessings He bestows upon us which we cannot count or afford to forget.

الله - A name from the names of His [The Most Blessed and High] that all His other names refer and return back to (the origin). This name refers back to His Lordship and the worship for the entire creation.

This worship is directed to Allah's perfection and giving it its rights in its fullest sense. Worship is which one submits and humbles themselves to. It shows us that the servitude of the slave requires faith in his Lord [The Most High].

القديم - He is the first and there was nothing before Him. This is solely for Allah and was mentioned here at the beginning to be the most suitable place of reminding us. It is not correct to acknowledge the name 'Al Qadeem' as a specific name of Allah's beautiful names and attributes.

The author [May Allah have mercy on him] mentions in his explanation of *Aqeedah Tahaweeyah* 'As for this title of *Al Qadeem* regarding the names of Allah then it is well-known and used amongst the people of dialectical theology (*Ahl Al Kalaam*) but opposed by others from the righteous predecessors (*Salaf As-Saliheen*) and those who came after such as Ibn Hazm.' There is no doubt that it would be the case if it is used to mean 'precedence' however in all the sayings of language 'Al Qadeem' refers to the definition of 'old'.

The names of Allah are the most beautiful that direct to specific prayers and worship used for praising Him. The word Pre-Eternal (Al Qadeem) is an exact title which does not relate to anything else except as a name of Allah used for Him alone. The Islamic Law also presents another meaning of 'The First' (Al Awwal) which may be more suitable than Pre-Eternal (Al Qadeem) because the word gives more of a sense that everything after belongs to Him. The Author however followed the opinion of Al Qadeem over Al Awwal and Allah's names are the most beautiful and not just nice.

Had the Shaykh (Rahimullah) used the title for Allah as 'Al Qadeer Al Baari' (The Decreed Fashioner) it would have been better suited because the title of 'Al Qadeer' (The One that Decrees) is a specific name of Allah that is often repeated in the Quran. It is also the most appropriate title to join with 'Al Baari' (The Fashioner) due to His fashioning ultimately being His ability and power with everything and nothing is diminished in His heavens or on Earth without His permission. If Allah wants to create something, He decrees it with His knowledge, His wisdom and it is fulfilled meaning comes into existence by His supreme ability. This is why the most befitting name for the opening line of poetry is 'Al Qadeem' which is preferred over the rest of the titles suggested.

We will conclude on this point here and Allah knows best.

الْبَارِي - This is another tremendous name of Allah, glorified and majestic is He. It has been established in the Quran with the meaning of the Creator of all creatures, the Originator of the universe and present before anything ceased to exist.

ثُمَّ صَلاَتُه - The praises and prayers of Allah [The Perfect, The High].

عَلَى الْمُخْتَار – Upon Muhammad Ibn Abdullah ﷺ.

الْمُخْتَار - The chosen one, Allah revealed:

﴿اللَّهُ يَصْطَفِي مِنَ الْمَلَائِكَةِ رُسُلًا وَمِنَ النَّاسِ إِنَّ اللَّهَ سَمِيعٌ بَصِيرٌ﴾

{Allah chooses messengers from Angels and from the mankind, indeed, Allah is Hearing and Seeing} (Al Hajj: 75)

Allah also says:

﴿وَرَبُّكَ يَخْلُقُ مَا يَشَاءُ وَيَخْتَارُ ۗ مَا كَانَ لَهُمُ الْخِيَرَةُ ۚ سُبْحَانَ اللَّهِ وَتَعَالَىٰ عَمَّا يُشْرِكُونَ﴾

{Allah creates what He wills and chooses; not for them was the choice. Exhalted is Allah and high above what they associate with Him} (Al Qasas: 68)

Muhammad ﷺ is the best of Allah's creation and the praise upon him is of the highest degree.[5]

[5] Abu Aaliyah (Rahimullah) states: The praise upon him stems from the angels and the praise of the angels is a supplication: Collected by Bukharee

وَبَعْدُ هَاكَ سِيرَةَ الرَّسُولِ مَنْظُومَةً مُوجَزَةَ الْفُصُولِ

Here's the life of the Messenger of our Lord

in precise divided chapters that we'll explore.

وَبَعْدُ - After praising Allah and sending peace and blessings upon the Messenger Alayhis Salaam.

هَاكَ - Take

سِيرَةَ الرَّسُولِ – Biography linguistically[6] means a good path or an evil one. This seerah is the path observing the biography of the Prophet Muhammad which is the purest and is specifically dedicated to him ﷺ. There was never anyone like him and there never will be the likes of him. The purpose of preserving the biography of the Messenger of Allah ﷺ in its authentic form is by way of learning the events that shaped the history of the Prophet ﷺ from his birth to his right of the highest companionship of Allah (the Most High).

الرَّسُولِ - Muhammad, the seal of the Prophets and the Imam for the first and the last ﷺ.

مَنْظُومَةً - The composer of the poem collected, authored, compared and

[6] Lisaan Al Arab (389/4)

connected verses together in this work with its rhytmtic style and purposeful meaning.

One of the benefits of this style is that it is precise and easy to commit to memory. This style was also used by the people of knowledge with relation to deriving rules from the Islamic Law. Their rhythm, series and beautiful verses encourage the students of knowledge to practice their words.

مُوجَزَةً - It is abridged which can be followed without distorting any of its meaning. Indeed, this short poem is comprised of a hundred main verses from various topics contained within this biography ﷺ and nothing is mentioned in this poetry except that it is soundly reported.

الْفُصُولِ - The sequence of the poem and the order of its events that are mentioned in the statements of the seerah are to be recited. Additionally, it does not provide any commentary from the author between each set of verses but rather it continues along the journey of the blessed life of the Messenger of Allah ﷺ.

وَلِدُهُ فِي عَاشِرِ الْفَضِيلِ   رَبِيعِ الأَوَّلِ عَامَ الْفِيلِ

Born in the days of the virtuous ten

Rabee al Awwal, the year elephant

لَكِنَّمَا الْمَشْهُورُ ثَانِي عَشْرِهِ   فِي يَوْمِ الاِثْنَيْنِ طُلُوعَ فَجْرِهِ

The twelth day, by far the most famous

Monday's rising of dawn amazingly gracious

وَوَافَقَ الْعِشْرِينَ مِنْ نَيْسَانَا   وَقَبْلَه حَيْنُ أَبِيهِ حَانَا

Corresponding to April on the 20th day

before this event his father passed away

The Shaykh (Rahimullah) mentions in these three verses issues relating to the birth of the Messenger of Allah ﷺ which many of the biographies of the Prophet also begin with.

مَوْلِدُه - The birth of the Prophet ﷺ.

فِي عَاشِرِ الْفَضِيل رَبِيعِ الأَوَّلِ - The tenth day of the month Rabee Al Awwal.

عَامَ الْفِيلِ - This is a well-known year which is named the year of the elephant. Here we examine the story of Abrahaa who marched towards Makkah to destroy Allah's house, the Ka'bah. Allah said:

﴿أَلَمْ تَرَ كَيْفَ فَعَلَ رَبُّكَ بِأَصْحَابِ الْفِيلِ۝أَلَمْ يَجْعَلْ كَيْدَهُمْ فِي تَضْلِيلٍ۝
وَأَرْسَلَ عَلَيْهِمْ طَيْرًا أَبَابِيلَ۝تَرْمِيهِم بِحِجَارَةٍ مِّن سِجِّيلٍ۝
فَجَعَلَهُمْ كَعَصْفٍ مَّأْكُولٍ﴾

{Have you not considered how your Lord dealt with the companions of the elephant, did he not make their plan into misguidance? and He sent against them birds in flocks, striking them with stones of hard clay and He made them like eaten straw} (Surah al-Fil)

It was in this year which was known as 'The Year of the Elephant'. The Arabs used to reminisce and talk about these stories with such names to remember historical events that took place in those earlier years.

لَكِنَّمَا الْمَشْهُورُ ثَانِي عَشْرِهِ - The 12th day by far the most famous meant that this was the day of the birth of the Messenger of Allah ﷺ. It took place in the month Rabee' Al Awwal and is very important to highlight. There is a difference of opinion on the actual birth date of the Prophet ﷺ whether he was born in this month or not. Here it is mentioned on the 12th day which seems to be the most common stance amongst the people of knowledge.

It is said by some that the Prophet ﷺ was born on the 8th day and others quote other dates.[7]

---

[7] Research: Bidaayah wal Nihaayah 376-374/3

This differing is also reported by Imam Al Albanee (Rahimullah) in his book *'Saheeh al-Seerah'* and in the great works of *'Al Bidaayah wa Nihayaah'* by Imam ibn Katheer (and they are all connected without chains of narrations). With revision its weight is held from the strength from the science of hadeeth. There is the exception of other references that describe the 8th day of his birth which is the narration of Maalik and his authentic chain linking back to Muhammad Bin Jubair Bin Mut'im who was an illustrious tab'iee (student of a companion). This was also verified by the historians of the past and those people who are relied upon. Imam Al Albanee also said that the majority agrees on the 12th day and this is the correct opinion and Allah knows best.[8]

All of these quotes are the variations of opinions present today on the birthday of the Prophet ﷺ. These evidences state that he was born in the night also. We do not attach any Islamic law to this but if there were to be some legislation connected to it or action to be implemented with this date there would be far greater differences of opinions amonst the scholars of knowledge. Whoever insists that the Prophet was born on such and such single day then the reply is that no supporting evidences which show this.

عَامَ الْفِيلِ – The Year of the Elephant.

This phrase directs us to what Imam Al Haakim narrates in his '*Mustadrak*'[9] that Ibn Abbas (RadhiyAllahu Anh) said: 'The Prophet was born in the Year of the Elephant'. Imam Haakim says that this narration is authentic with the condition (to asses the narration's grade) of the two

[8] Sahih Seerah Al Nabaweeyah, p.13
[9] No. 4239

shaykhs whom did not narrate this. Imam Dhahabi said: 'It is upon the condition of Muslim'.[10]

One of the narrations stems from Ibn Is'haq, Imam Haakim and others who reported that Qais Ibnu Makhramah (RadhiyAllahu Anh) said:

"The Messenger of Allah and I were both born in the Year of the Elephant and we are 'lidtaan' (born on the same day and time)[11]
It can be said 'so and so is the 'lidtaan' of so and so' meaning that two people were born at the same time.[12] The Prophet ﷺ was born in the Year of the Elephant and there is a difference whether he was born after the story of the elephant or not. The correct stance is that he was born after this event of a period of fifty days.[13]

فِي يَوْمِ الاِثْنَيْنِ طُلُوعَ فَجْرِه

Monday's rising of dawn amazingly gracious

The Prophet Muhammad ﷺ was born on a Monday as established in the authentic hadith from the narration of Imam Muslim[14].

Abu Qatadah Al Ansaree (RadhiyAllahu Anh) said: The Prophet was asked about fasting on Monday's in which he replied "It was this day that

[10]Authenticated also by Al Albanee in 'Saheeh Al Seerah p13. Research 'As Saheehah no. 3152

[11] Seerah Al Nabaweeyah ibn Is'haaq (99/1). Mustadrak Haakim (603/2). Authentic hadith on the condition of Muslim and he didn't narrate it. Al Albanee classified this hadeeth has Hassan 'Saheeh As-Seerah' p.13. See 'Silsillah As-Saheehah (3152)

[12] It is said that the 'lidda' of so and so is being brought up at the same time i.e born at the same time. The ت substitutes the و (Arabic grammar). See: Lisaan Al Arab (467/3)

[13] See Bidaayah wa Nihaayah (380/3)

[14] Muslim (1162)

I was born and the day I (will) was sent or it was revealed to me (i.e the message)". So it was the Monday that he ﷺ was born, the day he was sent, additionally it is the day in which he migrated from Makkah to Madeenah and the day he reached Madeenah. Monday is the day that he departed from this world ﷺ; it is also in this series of events in which the author will mention the order of these occurances.

وَوَافَقَ الْعِشْرِينَ مِنْ نَيْسَانَا - Corresponding with the 20th April, gregorian.

The word 'Neeysaan' also means April which is the fourth month of the solar calendar; As-Suhaylee reported this also in '*Rawadhat Al Anf*'. Mathematicians have also said: 'We can confirm this was the month that the Prophet was born and there were twenty days in which passed of this month.

وَقَبْلَه حَيْنُ أَبِيهِ حَانَا - Before this (event) his father passed away.

Intentional in his wording of 'وَقَبْلَه' meaning before regarding the birth of the Prophet ﷺ his father was alive. His father passed away whilst he ﷺ was in the womb of his mother. The word الحين refers to the stage of punishment after a person dies as stated in '*Al Qamoos*' and others.

The people of knowledge have differed concerning when the Prophet's father died. Was it while he was in the womb of his mother or after he was born? The correct view is that he died whilst the Prophet ﷺ was in the womb and he entered this world without any father making him an orphan child. Allah mentions this in the Quran and states:

﴿أَلَمْ يَجِدْكَ يَتِيمًا فَآوَىٰ﴾

{Did He (Allah) not find you (Oh Muhammed) an orphan and give you refuge?} (Surah Dhuha: 6)

وَبَعْدَ عَامَيْنِ غَدَا فَطِيمَا   جَاءَتْ بِهِ مُرضِعُهُ سَلِيمَا

Two years later of initial weaning

she returned with him in a condition that was pleasing

حَلِيمَةٌ لِأُمِّهِ وَعَادَتْ   بِهِ لِأَهْلِهَا كَمَا أَرَادَتْ

Halimah, to his mother and with him returned

back to her family as desired and yearned

وَبَعْدَ عَامَيْنِ - Two years after his birth ﷺ.

غَدَا - The weaning period began.

فَطِيمَا – He was weaned off breast feeding. This weaning period lasted for two complete yearly cycles. Allah explains:

﴿وَالْوَالِدَاتُ يُرْضِعْنَ أَوْلَادَهُنَّ حَوْلَيْنِ كَامِلَيْنِ لِمَنْ أَرَادَ أَنْ يُتِمَّ الرَّضَاعَةَ﴾

{Mothers may breastfeed for two complete years for whoever wishes to complete the nursing period} (Al Baqarah: 233)

جَاءَتْ بِهِ مُرضِعُهُ سَلِيمَا - A woman advanced to Makkah to the Prophet's mother. Muhammad ﷺ was sound and healthy, he was not stricken with any disease and she did not complain about any illnesses he had. His physique indicated he was well and he held strong genes.

حَلِيمَة - Halima Bint Abi Thuweeb Al Sa'deeyah was the wet nurse of the Prophet ﷺ. It was debated whether she and her husband were Muslims[15].

لِأُمِّه - To his mother (Amina) living in Makkah.

وَعَادَتْ بِهِ لِأَهْلِهَا - Halima returned with the Prophet ﷺ to her family. She was very astonished by his blessed nature and all the good he came with. Amazing and miraculous things took place which she never experienced before with any other child. The way he ﷺ breast fed was not like any of the other younger children.

She later took him back to his mother to convince her for him to stay longer under her care. It is written in other sources that she hinted (to his mother) that they had great weather where she looked after him. To her advantage his mother feared a plague that was prevelant in Makkah at the time along with other diseases that may affect his health. His mother

[15] See: Zaad Al Maad (83/1) and Subul Al Huda wal Rashaad (465/1)

ﷺ agreed to her request and he returned with Halimah back to her place of residence.[16]

كَمَا أَرَادَتْ - That his mother wanted (his return) to see him.

فَبَعْدَ شَهْرَيْنِ انْشِقَاقُ بَطْنِهِ   وَقِيلَ بَعْدَ أَرْبَعٍ مِنْ سِنِّهِ

Two months later his chest was split

around four years old and a bit.

Here the author [Rahimullah] mentions the story of the splitting of the chest of the Prophet ﷺ for the first time. This happened two months after Halimah returned him to his mother. Some people have stated that this took place at his tender age of four years old.

Ibn Is'haq has commented [17] 'a person from the companions of the Prophet ﷺ said to him: "O Messenger of Allah inform us about yourself"

'Yes, I am the dua of my forefather Ibraheem and the good news from our brother, Isa. When my mother was pregnant with me, she saw a light eminating from her that radiated the castles and palaces of Ash Shaam and I was fostered by Bani Sa'd ibn Bakr. We explained that we were looking after small farm animals behind a building for two men wearing exceedingly white clothes carrying a bucket made from gold filled with ice. They opened my stomach, extracted my heart and removed any black harmful clot in there. They then washed my heart and my stomach

[16] See: Seeratil Nabaweeyah of ibn Hishaam (177-179/2)
[17] Seerah Ibn Hishaam (181/1)

with the ice till it was cleansed. One of them said to his friend 'weigh him against ten people of his nation' so they weighed me and I outweighed them. Then they said 'against a hundred people of his nation' then they weighed me and I outweighed them. They then said 'against a thousand people', they weighed me and I outweighed them. One said 'leave him for by Allah, even if we weighed him against his whole nation he would outweigh them'. Ibn Kathir said 'This is a good, strong chain'.[18]

We also witness in *Sahih Muslim* the narration of Anas ibn Maalik that the Prophet ﷺ was visited by Jibreel whilst he was playing with other young boys. They took him and split open his heart, extracted it and removed the black clot and said 'This is the devil's fortune upon you'. Then they cleaned it from a golden dish with zamzam water inside and it was washed again to which it was returned back to his place. The young boy then ran to his mother and screamed: "Indeed Muhammad has been killed!". He was so shocked and scared his face changed colour. Anas added: "I saw many stitches on the chest of the Prophet ﷺ".

The stories of the splitting of the blessed chest of the Prophet are often repeated. Ibn Hajr mentions in 'Fat'h Al Baari' that the Prophet's chest was split three times.

The first incident took place in his childhood, it is explained 'He was cleared of all the evil matters and was freed from the devil's influence as remembered in the the previous hadith 'This is the devil's fortune upon you'. Secondly an event occured regarding his chest splitting when he was sent as a messenger and received many miracles of what was decreed by Allah towards strengthening his heart and absorbing all that which was pure. Finally, the last incident took place during the ascension to the heavens to prepare him for prayer and supplications. In the book '*Subul*

[18] Al Bidaayah wa Nihayah (413/3) Al Albanee classified it in Sahih Al Seerah (p17). See As-Saheehah (1045/1047)

Al Hudaa wal Rashaad' Saalihee describes 'the splitting of the Prophet's chest occurred four times, the second incident happened when he was ten years old'.

He had the most opening of hearts to people and was attentive to all who engaged with him. Ibn Al Qayyim [Rahimullah] said in '*Zaad Al Ma'ad'* that he ﷺ was guided calling towards Ihsaan with his charity and the enjoining of good. He ﷺ was the pinnacle of great character and spectacular in his personality. These characteristics were due to the great result of his heart being cleansed ﷺ. This is a summary of the opening of the Prophet's chest in relation to his prophethood and messengership and all that connects to it. His heart was also cleansed to extract the devil's fortune upon him (Hadh Al Shaytan). Elsewhere, the author has dedicated a full chapter on this explaining its great benefits and the reasons for the opening of the chest of the Prophet of Allah ﷺ.

وَبَعْدَ سِتٍّ مَعَ شَهْرٍ جَاءِ وَفَاةُ أُمِّهِ عَلَى الْأَبْوَاءِ

After six years and a month he faced

the passing of his mother in Abwaa'aa place

وَبَعْدَ سِتٍّ - Six years after his birth ﷺ.

مَعَ شَهْرٍ جَاءِ - A month later his mother visited her uncles from Bani Najjar and upon her return from Madinah to Makkah she passed away at a place called Abwaa'ah. Ibn Is'haq said[19]:

'Returning back to his mother afer being wet nursed by Halima this occurance commenced. The Prophet ﷺ was with his mother Amina bint Wahb and his grandfather Abdul Muttalib ibn Hishaam (May Allah protect him and provide for him as He wills from his miracliousness). He was six years old when his mother Amina passed away'.

Abdullah Bin Abi Bakr Bin Muhammad Bin Amro Bin Hazm narrated *'The mother of the Messenger of Allah ﷺ passed away in Abwaa'ah when he was six years old. It is an area between Makkah and Madinah where she was returning from a visit from her uncles of Bani Adiy bin Najjar and passed away on route back to Makkah'*.

It is reported by Imam Ahmad on the authority of Buraidah Bin Haseeb [May Allah be pleased with him] that he said:

"I went out with the Messenger of Allah until we reached Waddan and he said *'Stay here until I come back to you'.* Then he returned back to us later on (heavy with emotion) and said *"Indeed I have visited the grave of my mother and I asked my Lord for her intercession in which He denied me and I used to prevent you from visiting the graves but now visit them".*[20]

On the report of Imam Muslim that Abu Hurayrah narrates:

The Prophet visited his mother's grave and wept which caused us to cry also. He asked permission from his Lord to seek forgiveness for her but

[19] Seerah Nabaweeyah; Ibn Hishaam (182-183/1)
[20] Musnad 23017

he was prevented from doing so. Then I sought permission to visit his mother's grave and he gave me permission. He advised usby saying *"visit the graves for indeed it is a reminder for death"*.[21]

وَجَدُّه لِلْأَبِ عَبْدُ الْمُطَّلِبْ   بَعْدَ ثَمَانٍ مَاتَ مِنْ غَيْرِ كَذِبْ

His grandfather Abdul Mutallib died on this date

no rumour it was when the Prophet was eight

وَجَدُّه لِلْأَبِ عَبْدُ الْمُطَّلِبْ - Abdul Mutallib was the guardian of the Prophet ﷺ after his father passed away. He ﷺ was very virtuous amongst Abdul Mutallib's sons and children sitting with him in his circles and was very popular in his eyes.

بَعْدَ ثَمَانٍ مَاتَ[22] - He passed away eight years after the birth of the Prophet ﷺ. This was approximately two years after the death of the Prophet's mother Amina.[23]

He passed away eight years after the birth of the Prophet ﷺ. This was approximatley two years after the death of the Prophet's mother Amina.[24]

[21] Sahih Muslim 976
[22] A hundred
[23] Seerah Nabaweeyah ibn Hishaam (183/1)
[24] Seerah Nabaweeyah ibn Hishaam (183/1)

مِنْ غَيْرِ كَذِبْ - It was a famous incident that was mentioned in the biography of the Prophet ﷺ. Ibn Is'haq said '*When the Prophet reached eight years old his grandfather Abdul Mutallib passed away*'.

ثُمَّ أَبُو طَالِبٍ الْعَمُّ كَفَلْ خِدْمَتَهُ ثُمَّ إِلَى الشَّامِ رَحَلْ

Then with Abu Taalib, his uncle of protection

proceeded on a trip in the Shaam direction

وَذَاكَ بَعْدَ عَامِهِ الثَّانِي عَشَرْ وَكَانَ مِنْ أَمْرِ (بَحِيرَا) مَا اشْتَهَرْ

Then that year was the twelfth of his age

something occured, that to amaze

ثُمَّ أَبُو طَالِبٍ الْعَمُّ كَفَلْ خِدْمَتَهُ - While Abdul Muttalib was alive he instructed Abu Taalib to be the guardian of the Prophet ﷺ. He was the brother of the Prophet's father Abdullah. Abu Taalib was well-known for his concern and care over the Prophet thus becoming his protector. Whoever reads the biography of the Messenger will find Abu Talib being a distinguishing factor for the victory of the Prophet ﷺ. Although he persisted with aiding and sustaining the Prophet he continued his life as a non-Muslim and died upon disbelief.

Ibn Is'haq mentions that after the death of his grandfather Abdul Mutallib he ﷺ resided with his uncle Abu Taalib as a trust of the will left because his brother was Abdullah (the Prophet's father). Their mother Fatimah Bint Amro said: *"It was Abu Taalib who was left with the responsibility of the Messenger of Allah and was summoned to respect this instruction (given by Abdul Mutallib)"*[25].

ثُمَّ إِلَى الشَّامِ رَحَل - Here is the first trip the Prophet ﷺ took to Shaam with his uncle Abu Taalib in the early years of his life. During this trip Abu Talib kept him under close supervision and care.

Translator's note [26]

وَذَاكَ بَعْدَ عَامِهِ الثَّانِي عَشَر - When the Prophet ﷺ reached twelve years old.

وَكَانَ مِنْ أَمْرِ (بَحِيرَا) - They met a monk (Raahib).

مَا اشْتَهَرْ - Some great news and signs approached them.

Ibn Katheer says 'The Prophet ﷺ went out with his uncle Abu Taalib on a business trip to Shaam when he was twelve years old. This was his way of showing kindness towards him plus there was nobody to look after him ﷺ if he were to remain in Makkah. His uncle did not have any other person to guard and watch over the Prophet ﷺ as mentioned by Imam Tirmidhee in '*Al Jamiah*' from a chain where its men are from the intellectuals'.

---

[25] See: Bidaayah wa Nihaayah (432/3). Seerah Nabaweeyah, Ibn Hishaam (195/1)
[26] The land of Shaam in today's modern age refers to the countries of Jordan, Palestine, Syria and Lebanon (Levantine).

A mile from a tree there was a monk by the name of Bahira who advised his uncle to turn back to Makkah because if the Jews were to spot the Prophet they would kill him immediately (due to Bahira informing that Muhammad will be a prophet). Similarly, there is a hadith that has been preserved and other narrations contain extentions of this event.

This great news is also found in '*Jaamiah Tirmidhee*'[27] from the narration of Abu Musaa Al Ash'aree that was reported from Hassan and Ibn Hajr who graded its chain to be strong[28]. Al Haakim, Bayhaqi and others from the people of knowledge have (also) graded it authentic.

وَسَارَ نَحْوَ الشَّامِ أَشْرَفُ الْوَرَى   فِي عَامِ خَمْسَةٍ وَعِشْرِينَ اذْكُرَا

Again to sham the noblest from all

in his twenty fifth year this event we recall

لِأُمِّنَا خَدِيجَةٍ مُتَّجِرَا   وَعَادَ فِيهِ رَابِحًا مُسْتَبْشِرَا

For our mother Khadijah he did trade

returned again happy with a profit made

[27] No. 3620

[28] Fat'h Al Baari (216/2) See: Al Mustadrak (616/2) Dalaa'il Al Nabaweeyah Bayhaqi (24/2). Saheeh Al Seerah Al Albanee p.31

فَكَانَ فِيهِ عَقْدُهُ عَلَيْهَا   وَبَعْدَهُ إِفْضَاؤُهُ إِلَيْهَا

Then the contract to her was dated

next the marriage consumated

Here the author describes three different occasions in these lines of poetry. The second trip the Prophet ﷺ travelled to Sham for the purpose of business employed under Khadijah (May Allah be pleased with her). She heard that he ﷺ was a good man, his manners were impeccable and was trustworthy and truthful. She loved dealing in business with him because she had wealth and he had a great business acumen therefore proceeding to Al Shaam once again.

وَسَارَ نَحْوَ الشَّامِ - A merchant with the wealth of Khadijah heading to Al Shaam (May Allah be pleased with her).

أَشْرَفُ الْوَرَى - The best amongst them in goodness, a great example and a leader to them ﷺ.

فِي عَامِ خَمْسَةٍ وَعِشْرِينَ اذْكُرَا - When he reached twenty five years old he left for Shaam a second time.

Al Hafidh ibn Katheer mentions 'This was the second occurence the Prophet ﷺ travelled to Shaam with the business of Khadijah Bint Khuwaylid accompanied by her slave Maysarah whom was given to him as a loan. Maysarah saw remarkable things from the Messenger of Allah ﷺ and returned to Khadijah to pose a suggestion to her of marrying the

Prophet ﷺ as a way of thanking Allah for all that she has. He ﷺ married Khadijah at the age of twenty-five and she was forty years of age.

لِأُمِّنَا خَدِيجَةٍ - The title 'The Mother of the Believers' begun after her marriage to the Prophet ﷺ.

Allah describes her in Al Quran:

﴿وَأَزْوَاجُهُ أُمَّهَاتُهُمْ﴾

{And his wives, "are in the position of", their mothers (i.e. the believers)} (Al Ahzaab: 6)

مُتَّجِرًا – He was a tradesman with a set up loan from Khadijah. This is what is known as 'Al Mudharabah' where one person injects money into the other person's business and the second works for it (set up loan).

وَعَادَ فِيهِ - He returned again on this journey with the loan from Khadijah (May Allah be pleased with her).

رَابِحًا - A merchant will find much success and profit on a journey like this hence he returned ﷺ.

مُسْتَبْشِرًا – Very joyful and happy that Allah made this affair easy for him and this entrepreneurial quest he followed through with.

فَكَانَ فِيهِ – This year was the 25th of the Prophet's life ﷺ.

عَقْدُهُ عَلَيْهَا وَبَعْدَهُ إِفْضَاؤُهُ إِلَيْهَا - The Prophet ﷺ contracted his marriage with Khadijah (May Allah be pleased with her).

This was his first marriage and he didn't marry any other woman until she passed away. She has special virtues and unique characteristics that were reported in the ahadeeth of Al Bukharee and Al Muslim[29].

Aishah narrates: "*There was no woman I was jealous of from the wives of the Prophet ﷺ except my jealousy of Khadijah even though I never saw her but because the Prophet would mention her often. Whenever he used to slaughter a sheep he would cut it into parts and send it to the friends of Khadijah. I said to him it is as if there is no woman in the world to you except Khadijah, he replied "Khadijah was such and such and I had children to her*".

وَوِلْدُهُ مِنْهَا خَلاَ إِبْرَاهِيمْ   فَالْأَوَّلُ الْقَاسِمُ حَازَ التَّكْرِيمْ

Except Ibraheem his children she bore

the first was Al Qasim honored and more

وَوِلْدُهُ مِنْهَا خَلاَ إِبْرَاهِيمْ - The word 'wulud' (children) is a general term contrary to the word 'walad' (boys). Similarly, 'usud' (lions and lionesses) compared to the term 'asad' (male lions) is general and the latter excludes the meaning of female gender.

Allah described in Al Quran:

﴿يُوصِيكُمْ اللَّهُ فِي أَوْلاَدِكُمْ لِلذَّكَرِ مِثْلُ حَظِّ الأُنثَيَيْنِ﴾

{Allah instructs you concerning your children; for the male what is equal to two females} (Al Nisaa: 11)

[29] Bukharee no. 3818, Muslim no.2425

مِنْهَا - From Khadijah (May Allah be pleased with her).

خَلاَ إِبْرَاهِيمْ - Except Ibraheem, his mother was Maria the Coptic.

فَالْأَوَّلُ الْقَاسِمُ - The first was Al Qaasim, this name was used as the Prophet's nickname Abul Qaasim because Qaasim was his first son.

حَازَ التَّكْرِيم - To possess and to bear honor.

وَزَيْنَبٌ رُقَيَّةٌ وَفَاطِمَةْ   وَأُمُّ كُلْثُومٍ لَهُنَّ خَاتِمَةْ

Zaynab, Ruqaiyah and Fatimah too

then Umm Kulthoom was the last of the few.

They were the four daughters of the Prophet ﷺ. They understood and followed Al Islam and migrated to Madinah.

Translator's note[30]

Ibn Sa'd recorded a narration in his '*Tabaqaat*'[31] stemming from Ibn Abbas 'The first child the Prophet ﷺ had was in Makkah before his migration; this was Al Qaasim. He used this as his nickname then Zaynab was born next. Ruqaiyah followed then Fatimah and Umm Kulthoom. Finally, Abdullah was born who was also called Al Tayeb and

[30] Some views held do not believe that all his daughters migrated to Al Madinah.
[31] (133/1)

Al Taahir and they all shared the same mother, Khadijah Bint Khuwaylid'.

وَأُمُّ كُلْثُومٍ لَهُنَّ خَاتِمَةْ - Umm Kulthoom was the youngest of the daughters of the Prophet ﷺ however there is a difference of opinion amongst the scholars on this matter.

Ibn Abdul Barr mentions in '*Al Isti'aab*'[32] :

'There is a difference of viewpoints on who was the youngest daughter of the Prophet ﷺ and a greater difference on who the oldest amongst them was. This contention (differing) is a very peculiar one because the well known authentic position is that Zaynab is the eldest'.

Ibn Hajr explains in his '*Fat'h*'[33] "*It is agreed on by both Bukharee and Muslim that her children included Al Qaasim who the Prophet used as his nickname (kunya). Al Qaasim died as an infant before the Prophet was sent as a messenger or possibly after. Khadijah's children were four: Zaynab, Ruqaiyah, Umm Kulthoom and Fatimah. It is claimed by some that Umm Kulthoom was younger than Fatimah.*"

وَالطَّاهِرُ الطَّيِّبُ عَبْدُاللهِ   وَقِيلَ كُلٌّ اسْمٍ لِفَرْدٍ زَاهِي

Then Abdullah was pure and right

their names shining brightly like a single light

[32] (486/3) Al Isaabah
[33] (162/7)

These titles Tahir and Tayib were nicknames and not the two last sons of the Prophet ﷺ.

وَقِيلَ كُلُّ اسْمٍ لِفَرْدٍ - Here is the last mentioning whether they (Tahir and Taiyyib) were two children or not.[34] These are only three single names of one son from the four he had ﷺ.

زَاهِي - Described as a beautiful brightness.

وَالْكُلُّ فِي حَيَاتِهِ ذَاقُوا الْحِمَامْ   وَبَعْدَهُ فَاطِمَةٌ بِنِصْفِ عَامْ

All in his life their souls did depart

after his was Fatimah with six months apart

لْكُلّ - For each of (his children).

فِي حَيَاتِهِ - In his lifetime ﷺ.

ذَاقُوا الْحِمَامْ - Death approached them. Some of his daughters died before the migration and others after the migration to Al Madinah. His daughter Fatimah however passed away after the death of her father, Allah's Apostle ﷺ.

[34] Ibn Hajr 'Fat'h' (162/7) Abdullah was born after the migration. They called him Al Tahir and Al Tayeb. Others say that they are two brothers of his that died at young ages.

وَبَعْدَهُ فَاطِمَةٌ بِنِصْفِ عَامْ - Her passing was six months after the Prophet ﷺ.

In the collection of Bukharee and Muslim[35] on the authority of Aishah, Fatimah lived for six months after the passing of the Prophet ﷺ.

Also [36]on the report on Aishah (May Allah be pleased with her) she said:

"Fatimah came walking in the manner of the Prophet ﷺ. The Prophet ﷺ said, 'Welcome, O my daughter.' Then he seated her to his right or to his left then whispered something privately to her and she wept. I asked her "Why are you weeping?" Then he whispered something else privately to her and she smiled. I said, "I have never seen anything like that which I have seen today, of joy so close to grief." I asked her what he had whispered and she told me "I would not disclose the secret of the Messenger of Allaah ﷺ". When the Prophet ﷺ passed away I questioned her again about this and she said he told me "Jibreel used to review the Qur'aan with me once every year, but this year he has reviewed it with me twice so I know that my appointed time (of death) is approaching and you will be the first of my family to join me." So I wept. Then he asked "Would it not please you to be the leader of the women of Paradise or the women of the believers?" So I smiled immensley.'"

وَبَعْدَ خَمْسٍ وَثَلاثِينَ حَضَرْ بُنْيَانَ بَيْتِ اللهِ لَمَّا أَنْ دَثَرْ

At thirty–five years, he was there with the others

building Allah's house until it was covered

[35] Bukharee no. 4241 & 4245. Muslim no. 1759
[36] Sahih Bukharee no. 6282, 3623. Muslim no. 2450

In this line of poetry, we have an attendance around the Prophet ﷺ. They were the idol worshippers who rebuilt the house of Allah (Ka'bah) when the Prophet reached twenty-five years of age.

Ibn Is'haq described '*When the Prophet was twenty-five years old the Quraysh gathered collectively for the reconstruction of the Ka'bah*.[37]

This rebuilding was due to rips and cracks that forumlated on the walls from a mighty flood that gushed forth in Makkah and damaged parts of the infrastructure which required new repairs. The Messenger of Allah ﷺ was present at this event with them and participated in carrying stones as mentioned in the Sahihayn.[38]

Narrated Jaabir ibn Abdullah (May Allah be pleased with him)

The Prophet Muhammad ﷺ went with Abbas to carry some stones. Abbas advised "Put your loincloth round your neck to protect you from the stones". (As he did that) the Prophet ﷺ fell to the ground and his eyes turned skyward. Later on he woke up and shouted "My bottom cloth...my bottom cloth". He wrapped himself in his bottom cloth. In another report states His loins were never seen afterwards.

وَحَكَّمُوهُ وَرَضُوا بِمَا حَكَمْ   فِي وَضْعِ ذَاكَ الْحَجَرِ الْأَسْوَدِ ثَمّ

Pleased and glad with the judgement they faced

placing the black stone in its rightful place

---

[37] Seeratil Nabaweeyah by Ibn Hishaam (210/1)

[38] Bukharee no. 3829, Muslim 340

A great disagreement erupted between the tribes of the Quraysh on who would place the black stone in its place. Each clan knew the sanctity of this rock, its virtue and status. Everyone wanted this noble responsibility but everyone severly defended their right to take up this great effort. After a solution was presented the tribes were pleased to lift this rock. This solution was given that caused the status and value of the Prophet ﷺ to be elevated and he praised for his great idea.

Ibn Is'haq writes '*The tribes of Quraysh gathered to place the black rock in its position, every tribe united together in their own groups. When it came to raising the rock to its specific fitting the Quraysh all desired to fulfill this task until there emerged a big conflict in which they had to discuss*[39]*. It got so heated that they were prepared to kill one another during this event. Banu Abd Al Daar brought forth a basin filled with blood and made a pact with Udai Bin Ka'b Bin Lo'ay who dipped their hands in and made an oath against death to protect the black stone; this was known as the 'blood lick' (to indicate their non fear of blood shed). The Quraysh agreed to stay three or five nights in the masjid to settle this matter. Some historians of hadeeth have said that Abaa Miah Bin Mughirah Bin Abdullah Bin Umar Bin Makhzoom; who was from the eldest of the whole Quraysh called out and said:*

"O People of the Quraysh! Make an agreement between yourselves on what you differ on. The first person that walks through the door of this masjid will judge this matter and you must obey". It just so happened that the first who stepped through the door was the Messenger of Allah ﷺ in whom they saw and said "It is the trustworthy one, we are pleased it is Muhammad". They gathered around him and presented their dilemma. The Prophet ﷺ called for a cloth in which they gave to him and he said "Raise this rock and place it in its position". Each tribe leader held a section (of the cloth) with the black stone upon it and

[39] The black Stone

raised it together and the Prophet ﷺ set the stone in its place with his very own hands".[10]

Ibn Is'haq mentions and has cited it from the narration of Imam Ahmad[11] that Mujahid narrated from Mawlaa concerning the one who built the Ka'bah in the days of ignorance (jahiliyah). He says one owner of an idol once told a story and said "I sculptured this (idol) with my very own hands and I used to worship other than Allah. I brought forward mouldy milk which I prepared myself and poured it over them (the idols). A dog then would come, lick the milk off and find a vacant area and urinate on it. We kept extending it until we reached the stone (black stone) and none of us could see it. It layed between all of our idols shaped like the head of a man.

The chief of the Quraysh said "*we will place* (the black stone) *in its place*" others said " *We will place it into position*". They said "*Appoint for us someone to judge the affair*" and it was agreed that the first man who enters will solve the dilemma. As Allah's Apostle ﷺ approached them they said '*It is the trustworthy one*! ' and explained to him their situation. He ﷺ called for a cloth and asked for the nobles amongst each tribe to step forward and take a piece to carry it together and he ﷺ fitted it into place himself.

وَبَعْدَ عَامِ أَرْبَعِينَ أُرْسِلاَ فِي يَوْمِ الاِثْنَيْنِ يَقِينًا فَانْقُلاَ

At 40 years he was inspired with truth

On a Monday with revelation as evident proof

[10] Seeratil Nabaweeyah ibn Hisham (214-215/1)

[11] Al Musnad no.15504. Al Albanee said in 'Sahih Al Seerah' p.45 that it is a Hassan hadith

وَبَعْدَ عَامِ أَرْبَعِينَ أُرْسِلا - Forty years elapsed until the Prophet ﷺ was revealed with the message informing that he has been brought as a mercy to mankind, a bearer of good news and a warner to the people. This was also reported by Ibn Abbas, Jibreel Bin Mut'im and others from the companions and the tabi'een and additionally collected by Imam Bukharee and Muslim[42].

Ibn Abbas shared "*The Prophet was given prophethood at the age of forty and was inspired with the revelation in Makkah for thirteen years until he made the migration to reside in Al Madinah. There he lived for ten years and died there at the age of sixty-three*".

فِي يَوْمِ الاِثْنَيْنِ - It was on a Monday that the revelation was sent down to him ﷺ.

يَقِينًا فَانْقُلا - This prophethood was revealed with certainty and truth, there is no dispute concerning his revelation. It is established in an authentic narration on the Prophet ﷺ that Imam Muslim collected.[43] Abu Qataadah Al Ansaaree may (Allah be pleased with him) said the Prophet was asked about fasting on a Monday, he replied "*This was the day I was born and the day I was sent with the Quranic revelation*".

فِي رَمَضَانَ أَوْ رَبِيعِ الْأَوَّلِ وَسُورَةُ اقْرَأْ أَوَّلُ الْمُنَزَّلِ

Rabee Al Awwal or Ramadan

the Chapter 'Read' was revealed from Quran

[42] Bukharee no.3902, Muslim no. 2351
[43] No. 1162

فِي رَمَضَانَ أَوْ رَبِيعِ الأَوَّلِ - There is a slight difference of opinion on the month the Quran was revealed upon the Prophet ﷺ and some contention that the day was a Monday. Ibn Al Qayyim (Rahimullah) states in his work '*Zaad Al Ma'aad*'[44] "There is no disagreement that the prophethood happened on a Monday. The scholar's views differ regarding the month that it was revealed (Surah Alaq). Some hold that it was the eighth day of Rabee Al Awwal forty-one years since the Year of the Elephant and this is the majority view. Others recollect (the first inspiration) was revealed in the month of Ramadan as Allah says in the verse in Al Quran:

﴿شَهْرُ رَمَضَانَ الَّذِي أُنْزِلَ فِيهِ الْقُرْآنُ﴾

{The month of the Ramadan was the month the Quran was revealed} (Al Baqarah: 185)

Ramadhan was the first time that Allah honoured and exaulted the Prophet ﷺ with the Quran. It is this specific point the majority do not believe to be correct.

The first group explain that the Quran was sent down in Ramadhan as one part to the 'Bayt Al-Izzah' or 'Bayt Al Ma'mur' (Sacred house in the seventh heaven) then sent it down in stages relating to different events over a period of twenty-three years.

Translators note [45]

[44] (77-78/1)

[45] Note: The scholars agree that the Quraan was sent down on Laylatul Qadr (The night of Power) in Ramadan. The debate lies regarding the first few verses from Surah Alaq (The Chapter of the Clot) when the Muhammad was informed he was a Prophet, did this take place in Ramadan also? The majority have stated that this occured in the month Rabee Al Awwal.

وَسُورةُ اقْرَأْ أَوَّلُ الْمُنَزَّلِ - This chapter (Al Alaq) was the first revealed unto the Messenger of Allah ﷺ as reported in the Sahihayn on the authority of 'Aishah[46] (May Allah be pleased with her).

ثُمَّ الْوُضُوءَ وَالصَّلاَةَ عَلَّمَهْ جِبْرِيلُ وَهْيَ رَكْعَتَانِ مُحْكَمَةْ

Ablution and prayer was what he was taught

by the mighty Jibreel two rakah sought.

This was a command from the earliest orders sent at the beginning of his prophethood. Ibn Is'haq describes[47] 'It was narrated to me by some of the people of knowledge that it was at this time when the prayer was ordered upon the Prophet ﷺ whilst he was at the highest point in Makkah. Jibreel prodded him to go Aqabah to the furthest valley and a spring gushed forth from the earth. Jibreel then made ablution and the Prophet watched how he prepared for the prayer, the Prophet followed and performed ablution the way he saw Jibreel doing it. Jibreel then rose to pray and the Prophet ﷺ prayed with him until Jibreel left. The Prophet ﷺ then returned to Khadijah (May Allah be pleased with her) and performed ablution so she may see how this ritual should be carried out. He then led her in the prayer just like Jibreel did with him'.

Suhaily narrates in '*Rawdhat Al Anf*'[48] that this hadith is broken regarding the seerah and has no basis concerning the rules and regulations of the Islamic Law. However, there is a narration stemming

[46] Bukharee no. 3 Muslim no. 170 / 171
[47] Seerah Nabaweeyah ibn Hishaam (272/1)
[48] (13/3)

back to Zaid Bin Harithah (the adopted son) which lifts the hadith's authenticity. There are other narrations from Abdullah Bin Lahiyah but is deemed as weak. The hadith of Zaid referred to is from the collection of Imam Ahmad, Ibn Majah, Haakim and others[49].

Narrated Zaid ibn Harithah, the Prophet ﷺ said '*Jibril taught me* (how to perform) *the ablution and he ordered me to sprinkle water underneath my garment lest a drop of urine is leaked.*'"

This is from the narration of Bin Lahiyah this and these narrations are supported by Imam Al Albanee in his '*Silsilah As-Saheehah*'.[50]

ثُمَّ مَضَتْ عِشْرُونَ يَوْمًا كَامِلَةْ   فَرَمَتِ الجِنَّ نُجُومٌ هَائِلَ

Next the elapse of twenty days

Shooting stars as Jinn left them afraid

ثُمَّ مَضَتْ عِشْرُونَ يَوْمًا - Twenty days after the Prophet received the revelation.

فَرَمَتِ الجِنَّ - Eavesdroppers from high places.

نُجُومٌ - Allah describes the Jinn like meteors guarding the skies:

[49] Al Musnad no. 17480, Ibn Majah no. 462, Al Mustadrak (217/3)
[50] No. 841

﴿وَأَنَّا لَمَسْنَا السَّمَاءَ فَوَجَدْنَاهَا مُلِئَتْ حَرَسًا شَدِيدًا وَشُهُبًا۝وَأَنَّا كُنَّا نَقْعُدُ مِنْهَا مَقَاعِدَ لِلسَّمْعِ ۖ فَمَن يَسْتَمِعِ الْآنَ يَجِدْ لَهُ شِهَابًا رَّصَدًا﴾

{And we have sought to reach the secrets of the heavens and we found it filled with powerful guards and burning flames. And we used to sit therein in position for hearing but whoever listens now will find burning flame lying in wait for him} (Al Jinn 8-9)

هَائِلَ - Stationed in horror, fearing the command in which they do not know what will approach next.

Ibn Al Jawzee says 'The scholars of seerah mention that the Quraysh saw shooting stars twenty days after the revelation to the Prophet ﷺ.'[51]

Imam Ahmad, Tirmidhee and others narrated from Ibn Abbas "*The jinn used to ascend through the heavens trying to listen about the revelation so when they heard a statement they added nine (lies) to it. The statement that they heard would be true while what they added was false. It was with the advent of the Messenger of Allah that they were prevented from their places. So they mentioned that to Iblis because the stars were not shot at this. Iblis said to them "This is nothing but an event that has occurred in the earth*".

He then casted out his armies and they found the Messenger of Allah standing in prayer between two mountains. Urwaa said "In Makkah" they (returned) to meet with him (Iblis) and informed him. He said 'This is the event that has happened on the earth.'[52]

[51] Siffatus Safwaa (1/85) See: Bad'a Al tareekh of Mat'har bin Taahir Al Maqdisee (144/4) Al Imtaa' Al Ismaa' of Al Miqreezy (6/5)
[52] Musnah Ahmad 2977. Tirmidhee 3324 who said it was a Hassan hadith and classified authentic by Al Albanee

ثُمَّ دَعَا فِي أَرْبَعِ[53] الْأَعْوَامِ بِالْأَمْرِ جَهْرَةً إِلَى الْإِسْلَامِ

In the fourth year he did preach

an open call to Islam was his speech

Here begins the start of his open dawah calling to Allah in the 4th year of his prophethood, prior to this his propagation to Islam was hidden. Ibn Al Qayyim (Rahimullah) said in *Zaad Al Ma'aad* '*before this year he called to Allah for three years in secret until a verse was instructed unto him'*.

﴿فَاصْدَعْ بِمَا تُؤْمَرُ وَأَعْرِضْ عَنِ الْمُشْرِكِينَ﴾

{And declare what you are commanded and turn away from the idol worshipper} (Al Hijr: 94)

This was the turning point for his dawah, warning his people against the enemy and to prepare for the upcoming difficulties till Allah permits them to make the two migrations.

وَأَرْبَعٌ مِنَ النِّسَا وَاثْنَا عَشَرْ مِنَ الرِّجَالِ الصَّحْبِ كُلٌّ قَدْ هَجَرْ

Four of the women left their state

with twelve male companions they did migrate

[53] It is recorded like this in many texts (four)

إِلَى بِلاَدِ الْحُبْشِ فِي خَامِسِ عَامْ   وَفِيهِ عَادُوا ثُمَّ عَادُوا لاَ مَلاَمْ

To Abysinnia in the year five

then returned once again a second time

Here both migrations to Abyssinia (Ethiopia) are mentioned.

وَأَرْبَعٌ مِنَ النِّسَا وَاثْنَا عَشَرْ مِنَ الرِّجَال - The number of migrants that departed the first time. There were four from the believing women accompanied by twelve men that set off for Abyssinia.

إِلَى بِلاَدِ الْحُبْشِ كُلٌّ قَدْ هَجَر - They all migrated to Abyssinia.

فِي خَامِسِ عَامْ - In the 5th year of the prophethood.

وَفِيهِ عَادُوا - They returned again in the same year.

عَادُوا - They travelled back to Makkah because news reached them that the situation there improved. They heard that the oppression and torment stopped against the Muslims but when they reached Makkah it was the complete opposite. Not all the companions that migrated to Abyssinia travelled back to Makkah, some of them remained.

ثُمَّ عَادُوا - Returning again to Abyssinia.

لاَ مَلاَمْ - Without any blame upon them.

ثَلاثَةٌ هُمْ وَثَمَانُونَ رَجُلْ وَمَعَهُمْ جَمَاعَةٌ حَتَّى كَمُلْ

Eighty–three from amongst the men

with a group of people they then went.

وَهُنَّ عَشْرٌ وَثَمَانٍ ثُمَّ قَدْ أَسْلَمَ فِي السَّادِسِ حَمْزَةُ الْأَسَدْ

With eighteen women the travel they faced

in the sixth year of Islam, Hamzah embraced

ثَلاثَةٌ هُمْ وَثَمَانُونَ رَجُلْ - Eighty-three men migrant men travelled back to Abysinnia the second time.

وَهُنَّ عَشْرٌ وَثَمَانٍ - There were eighteen women that migrated alongside them.

Ibn Al Qayyim (Rahimullah) expands on this whole incident in '*Zaad Al Ma'aad*[54] '*When the Muslims started to gain larger numbers the disbelievers became worried therefore oppressed the believers more severely, ultimately this was a great trial upon the believers. The Prophet* ﷺ *ordered them to migrate to Abysinnia and informed them "There is a king there who does not oppress his people" and thus the believers set off on their escape to this land with twelve men and four women. From them were Uthman ibn Affan and his wife Ruqaiyah, the daughter of the*

[54] (97-98/1)

Messenger of Allah ﷺ. They arrived in Abysinnia having the best of neighbours and surroundings.

The rumour reached them that the Quraysh had accepted Islam however this was not true. The companions returned to Makkah, upon arrival noticed that the oppression and tribulations were greater than before they left. Some of them who returned went back to Abyssinia while a party of the Quraysh continued to tortue the believers more (in Makkah).

When Abdullah Bin Masood (May Allah be pleased with him) entered Makkah he instructed the believers to go back to Abysinnia the second time, eighty-three men went and Ammar complained against the injustices happening to them. There were eighteen women that went alongside the men who stood before Najashi feeling safe in his land. The Quraysh dispatched Amr Bin Al Aas and Abdullah ibn Abi Rabiah to plot against the Muslims while they were with Najashi but Allah turned their plans back on them.

ثُمَّ قَدْ أَسْلَمَ فِي السَّادِسِ - After the Prophet ﷺ entered Daar Al Arqam Hamzah accepted Islam. It is also recorded that (Hamzah's conversion) took place in the 2nd year of the Prophethood'[55]

حَمْزَةُ الْأَسَدْ - Hamzah or 'Hamzah the Lion' was the uncle of the Prophet ﷺ and like a brother in the sense that (they were both suckled by the slave Thuwaybah). When he embraced Islam he was victorious for the religion and gave honor and confidence to the believers. After Hamzah it was Umar Ibn Al Khattab (May Allah be pleased with him) who

[55] See: Al Istiaab by Ibn Abd Al Birr (271/1) Al Isaabah by Ibn Hajr / Bidaayah wal Nihayah ibn Katheer (28-29/3)

embraced the faith a few days later and was a great assistance to Islam and the Muslims.

وَبَعْدَ تِسْعٍ مِنْ سِنِي رِسَالَتِهْ   مَاتَ أَبُو طَالِبَ ذُو كَفَالَتِهْ

After nine years since revelation

Abu Talib died a guard from his nation

وَبَعْدَه خَدِيجَةٌ تُوُفِّيَتْ   مِنْ بَعْدِ أَيَّامٍ ثَلاَثَةٍ مَضَتْ

Then Khadijah passed away

after his uncle by three days

In these two verses the author mentions the death of the uncle of the Prophet ﷺ Abu Talib and his wife Khadijah who both passed away in the 9th year of his message.

مِنْ سِنِي رِسَالَتِه - In the 9th year of his prophethood.

مَاتَ أَبُو طَالِبَ ذُو كَفَالَته - Abu Talib was the guardian over the Prophet ﷺ after his grandfather Abdul Mutallib, he was a protector of the Prophet ﷺ and a loving supporter.

وَبَعْدَه خَدِيجَةٌ تُوُفِّيَتْ – This is a famous position by the scholars of seerah (that Khadijah passed away after Abu Taalib).

Ibn Katheer explains in '*Al Bidaayah wa Nihayah*[56] '*the Prophet's uncle passed away then next followed Khadijah Bint Khuwaylid* (the Prophet's wife). Others adopted the position that her death was before his but the most common and famous stance is the first. Both were compassionate towards the Prophet. One was outwardly (Abu Taalib) and one was internally (Khadijah), he was a disbeliever and she is a truthful believer'. Ibn Is'haq says 'Khadijah and Abu Talib tasted death in the same year in which affected the Prophet ﷺ greatly with the passing of his dear wife whom was the pinnacle of truthfulness living with him when his uncle departed this world. Abu Talib was his defender, used his upper hand to prevent evil and harm coming to his nephew and was an aider to his people. Three years before the hijrah to Madinah Abu Talib convinced the Quraysh to stop the oppression on the Prophet ﷺ because he wasn't pleased with these attacks during his lifetime'.

مِنْ بَعْدِ أَيَّامٍ ثَلَاثَةٍ مَضَتْ - The people of knowledge do not differ that Abu Talib and Khadijah died in the same year, the disagreement falls with whom passed away first. The common opinion is that Khadijah passed away after Abu Talib by a period of three days.

Ibn Katheer says that Al Bayhaqi said "*it was relayed to me that Khadijah passed away three days after Abu Talib*". This is also mentioned in the book of Abdullah ibn Munduh '*Al Ma'rifah*' and from our Shaykh Al Hafidh Abu Abdullah.[57]

[56] (304/4)
[57] Al Murja As-Sabiq (312/4)

وَبَعْدَ خَمْسِينَ وَرُبْعٍ أَسْلَمَا   جِنُّ نَصِيبِينَ وعَادُوا فاعْلَمَا

After fifty and a quarter the Jinn accepted

returned to teach them they left affected

وَبَعْدَ خَمْسِينَ - Fifty years after his birth ﷺ.

وَرُبْع - A quarter of the year, the passing of three months.

أَسْلَمَا جِنُّ نَصِيبِينَ - When the Prophet ﷺ reached the age of fifty years old and three months some amongst the Jinn accepted his call. This was recorded by a scholar from those who documented the life and times of the Prophet ﷺ.

Ibn Al Jawzee states in '*Sifaatas Safwaa*[58] '*When the Prophet ﷺ reached the age of fifty years and three months old the Jinn approached him and accepted the faith of Islam*'.

It is also recited in '*Alfia'ah as Seerah*' by Al Hafidh Al Iraqee:

After fifty years passed and the four added, that year they came seeking

The Jinn were there and others while the prayer was being recited

They listened to the Quran and accepted the truth, and went back to their people conveying the message.

[58] (108/1)

This occurrence of the Jinn took place after he ﷺ left Taif. Ibn Katheer [Rahimullah] describes in his explanation of the Quran 'Muhammad Ibn Is'haq mentions a narration from Yazeed Bin Muawiyah from Muhammad ibn Ka'b Al Qardhee a story about this journey. He ﷺ supplicated for them [the people of Taif] and for their forefathers and this is a long narration. The supplication he made was **'O Allah to you I complain, my strength has been weakened and my resources are scarce'** until the end of this dua. When he departed them he ﷺ started to recite verses from the Quran at a palm tree in which some of the Jinn were listening attentively.

نَصِيبِينَ - With the fat'h pronunciation on the letter Noon. This is a city between Turkey and Syria.

وعَادُوا فَاعْلَمَ - They returned back to their families conveying the message and warning them. They were callers towards the tawheed of Allah as Allah mentions in Al Quran:

﴿وَإِذْ صَرَفْنَا إِلَيْكَ نَفَرًا مِّنَ الْجِنِّ يَسْتَمِعُونَ الْقُرْآنَ فَلَمَّا حَضَرُوهُ قَالُوا
أَنصِتُوا ۖ فَلَمَّا قُضِيَ وَلَّوْا إِلَىٰ قَوْمِهِم مُّنذِرِينَ﴾

{And mention when we directed you to a few amongst the Jinn listening to the Quran. And when they attended they said 'listen quietly' and when it was concluded they returned to their people as warners} (Al Ahqaaf: 29)

This is a clear evidence to show that the Prophet ﷺ was sent to mankind and the Jinn collectively.

ثُمَّ عَلَى سَوْدَةَ أَمْضَى عَقْدَهْ فِي رَمَضَانَ ثُمَّ كَانَ بَعْدَهْ

Then with Sawdah a contract spent

In Ramadan this was meant

عَقْدُ ابْنَةِ الصِّدِّيقِ فِي شَوَّالِ، وَبَعْدَ خَمْسِينَ وَعَامٍ تَالِ

Married Al Sideeq's daughter in the Shawwal days

at over fifty years of age

ثُمَّ عَلَى سَوْدَةَ - One example here illustrates the sympathy and compassion the Prophet ﷺ had was that he did not marry again until his wife Khadijah passed away and not whilst she was still alive. He then contracted a marriage with Sawdah Bint Zama'ah ibn Qais Al Qurayshi after a short period of time. Before this marriage she was with a man named Sakran ibn Amro (May Allah be pleased with him) and she migrated to Abysinnia. Shortly after her return back to Makkah with him he died. The Prophet ﷺ tied a wedding contract with Sawdah during the month of Ramadan before his migration to Al Madinah, it was said to be a period of two years before the hijrah although others mention three years.

Some of her unique virtues was sacrificing one of her days for Aishah (May Allah be pleased with her) out of the sheer love the Prophet ﷺ had for Aishah. She matured whilst living with the Prophet ﷺ and showed great persistence when divorce was presented to her. He ﷺ offered to divorce her but she strongly insisted to stay married to him to be his wife in this world and in the next life.

Translator's note[59]

ثُمَّ كَانَ بَعْدَه - After this marital contract was complete.

عَقْدُ ابْنَةِ الصِّدِّيقِ فِي شَوَّالِ - This was Aishah Bint Abi Bakr Al Sideeq (May Allah be pleased with her and upon her father and all of the companions). He married her in the month of Shawwal before the migration to Madinah, some say by two years and others mention three. Another party of scholars debated that this happened when they first reached Madinah when she was nine years old.

Some of her virtues:

- She was the most loved wife by the Prophet ﷺ.
- He never married another young woman other than her.
- Revelation came to the Prophet whilst he was with her in privacy.
- She was freed by Allah from the accusations made against her at the event of Al Ifk (blaming her of fornication) whereby verses were revealed in her defense.
- She was the most learned in rulings (Al Fiqh) from the women, rather from the entire Ummah.
- The Prophet passed away in her home with his head between her chin and her chest.

[59] There is no doubt that the Messenger of Allah's request was one out of compassion and consideration. He judged that her feelings may be scarred out of her constant attempts to compete with his other younger wives therefore offered her the freedom of divorce to eleviate any pain she may face emotionally.

وَبَعْدَ خَمْسِينَ وَعَامٍ تَال

...at over fifty, years of age.

أُسْرِيْ بِهِ وَالصَّلَوَاتُ فُرِضَتْ   خَمْسًا بِخَمْسِينَ كَمَا قَدْ حُفِظَتْ

Ascended to where the prayer was obliged

then it was known as fifty– five

This incident describes the affair after the night journey.

وَبَعْدَ خَمْسِينَ وَعَامٍ تَال - This occurance happened fifty one years since the birth of the Prophet ﷺ. Ibn Al Jawzee explains 'When the Prophet ﷺ reached the age of fifty-one and nine months old he was sent on the night journey.'

أُسْرِيْ بِهِ - From Makkah to the Holy Masjid in Jerusalem (Bayt Al Maqdis). In this same night he ﷺ ascended to the seventh heaven where he received the command of the five daily prayers which were reduced from fifty prayers to five.

خَمْسًا - Five to be performed in action and بِخَمْسِينَ in the reward of fifty prayers.

كَمَا قَدْ حُفِظَتْ - This occurance is established and recorded in the authentic tradition of the Prophet ﷺ[60].

Al Hafidh ibn Katheer (Rahimullah) highlights 'The Prophet ascended on the night journey in his physical bodily form as was attested by the companions and the scholars. This was a journey he took from Masjid Al Haram to the Holy Mosque in Jerusalem to lead the prayer there. He then flew (via Buraaq)[61] through the sky of the dunya and then the next, then the third, then the next, then the fifth until he reached the seventh sky in which he saw the prophets and messengers at different stages of his ascention. He kept on rising until he reached Sidrat Al Muntahaa (the furthest boundary of the lote tree) where he saw Jibreel in his true form just as Allah created him, Allah commanded him the five daily prayers in that night'.[62]

وَالْبَيْعَةُ الْأُولَى مَعَ اثْنَيْ عَشَرَا مِنْ أَهْلِ طَيْبَةَ كَمَا قَدْ ذُكِرَا

Twelve took the pledge willing and not ordered

from the city of Taybah as recorded

وَالْبَيْعَةُ الْأُولَى - Here is the first pledge of Al Aqabah (where the believers swore an oath of allegiance to Allah's messenger at the place called Aqabah) with twelve men from them accepting the faith.

[60] The story of Al Israa wal mi'raaj is mentioned its extended version in the Sahihayn. Bukharee no. 3342 / Muslim no 263 from the hadith of Anas ibn Abi Dharr (May Allah be pleased with him)

[61] A heavenly riding beast

[62] Al Fusool fi Seeratil Rasool (p.69)

مِنْ أَهْلِ طَيْبَةَ - They were the people of Taybah (the old name Al Madinah).

كَمَا قَدْ ذُكِرَ - As was recorded in the biography of the Prophet ﷺ. Ibn Is'haq describes 'When Allah wished that His religion become apparent, His prophet ﷺ be honoured and his followers be glorified he sent out His Prophet ﷺ who received a man from the Ansaar who introduced himself to the Arabian tribes as was the custom to do every season. This man came to the pledge of Al Aqabah with a group of men from the tribe of Khazraj whom Allah wanted goodness for. These men responded to the call that the prophet ﷺ was proclaiming, they believed in him and left to convey this message to their people'.

He (Ibn Is'haq) also added 'When these men reached back home at Al Madinah they explained whom the Messenger of Allah was and this call of Islam until it became widespread. There was not a place nor home in Madinah where the call hadn't reached. In the same month of the following year twelve men came to take the pledge which was called the first pledge of Al Aqabah. They swore an oath of allegiance to Allah and His Messenger along with the pledge of the women, this was before the order of warefar was mandated upon them'.[63]

What is meant by 'The Pledge of the Women' is which is described in surah Mumtahinah[64] and in the Sahihayn[65].

Narrated Ubaadah ibn Saamit (May Allah be pleased with him) said 'We gave the pledge of allegiance to him that we would not worship anything

[63] See: Seerah Al Nawaweeyah, Ibn Hishaam (452-454/2)
[64] Verse 12
[65] Sahih Bukharee no. 3893/ Muslim no. 1709

other than Allah, steal, commit illegal sexual intercourse, kill a person that Allah has made illegal except rightfully or rob one other. We would not be promised Paradise if we did the above sins, if we did Allah would give His Judgment concerning it.

وَبَعْدَ ثِنْتَيْنِ وَخَمْسِينَ أَتَى سَبْعُونَ فِي الْمَوْسِمِ هَذَا ثَبَتَا

In his fifty second year they came for a reason

seventy men in this blessed season

مِنْ طَيْبَةٍ فَبَايَعُوا ثُمَّ هَجَرْ مَكَّةَ يَوْمَ اثْنَيْنِ مِنْ شَهْرِ صَفَرْ

Another pledge from Taybah then he migrated

Makkah on a Monday, Safar dated

وَبَعْدَ ثِنْتَيْنِ وَخَمْسِينَ - Fifty two years since the birth of the Prophet Muhammad ﷺ.

أَتَى - Came ﷺ.

سَبْعُونَ - Seventy men in the Hajj season.

هَذَا ثَبَتَ - What was established in the authentic narrations of hadith.

مِنْ طَيْبَةٍ فَبَايَعُوا – The men of Taybah (Madinah) took the second pledge of Al Aqabah in the presence of the Prophet ﷺ.

ثُمَّ هَجَرْ - Then the Prophet ﷺ made his migration heading Al Madinah

مَكَّةَ يَوْمَ اثْنَيْنِ مِنْ شَهْرِ صَفَر - One opinion states his migration in the month of Safar but others have also confirmed the month Rabee Al Awwal. Ibn Katheer mentions in '*Bidayah wa Nihayah*'[66] 'the Prophet ﷺ migrated in Rabee Al Awwal in the 13th year of his sending and this was on a Monday as Imam Ahmad also collects.[67]

Ibn Abbas narrates "*Your Prophet was born on a Monday, migrated from Makkah to Madinah on a Monday, was given the prophethood on a Monday, he entered Madinah on a Monday and finally passed away on a Monday.*"

فَجَاءَ طَيْبَةَ الرِّضَا يَقِينَا	إِذْ كَمَّلَ الثَّلاثَ وَالْخَمْسِينَا

Alas he arrived, the land full of pleasure indeed

at the year of his age, fifty-three

[66] (443-444/4)

[67] No. 2506. Its wording: The Prophet was born on a Monday and was received the revelation on a Monday and died on a Monday and migrated from Makkah to Madinah on a Monday and entered Madinah on a Monday and lifted the black stone on a Monday. A chain of narration linking back to Abdullah Bin Lahiyah.

فِي يَوْمِ الاِثْنَيْنِ وَدَامَ فِيهَا   عَشْرَ سِنِينَ كَمَلَتْ نَحْكِيهَا

There on a Monday he settled to live

for ten whole years, this story we'll give

فَجَاءَ طَيْبَةَ - He arrived at Taybah currently known Madinah Al Nabawiyah (The City of The Prophet).

الرِّضَا - Pleased with what Allah decreed for him. **يَقِينَا** - which was established and proven in the seerah.

إِذْ كَمَّلَ الثَّلاَثَ وَالْخَمْسِينَ - When fifty three years of his life elapsed

فِي يَوْمِ الاِثْنَيْنِ - He entered Madinah on a Monday. Al Haakim said '*There were accounts that the Prophet ﷺ left Makkah on a Monday and entered Madinah on a Monday*'[68].

وَدَامَ فِيهَا - He resided there until he departed this world ﷺ.

كَمَلَتْ - Completed in its entirety.

نَحْكِيهَ - This is proven on what was transmitted from the narrations of ahadeeth. Ibn Abbas said "The Prophet ﷺ was sent to humanity at the

[68] Ibn Hajr in 'fat'h Al Baari' (236/7) and Al Saalihee in 'Subul Al Hudaa wal Rashaad' (360/3)

age of fourty, he resided in Makkah for thirteen years where he received revelation. He was then commanded to migrate to Al Madinah where he lived for ten years and passed away at the age of sixty-three".[69]

أَكْمَلَ فِي الأُولَى صَلاَةَ الحْضَرِ　　　مِنْ بَعْدِ مَا جَمَّعَ فَاسْمَعْ خَبَرِي

A resident's prayer in the first year being certain

after they gathered hearing the sermon

أَكْمَلَ فِي الأُولَى – In the 1st year of the hijrah (prophetic migration).

Translator's note[70]

صَلاَةَ الحْضَرِ - They performed the prayers Dhur, Asr and Ishaa as four units. In the Sahihayn [71] Aishah narrates "The prayers were mandated as two units of prayer until the Prophet migrated to Madinah and instructed them to pray them as four units but the traveller's prayer remained the same (as two units).

مِنْ بَعْدِ مَا جَمَّعَ – The Friday prayers were established in Madinah after the prophetic hijrah.

فَاسْمَعْ خَبَرِي – They listened attentively to the sermon with sheer acceptance of its reminder. Ibn Katheer (Rahimullah) narrates 'When the Prophet departed from the area Al Qubaa on his she camel Qaswaa

[69] Primarily reported

[70] The Hijrah marks the beginning of the Islamic Calendar. Its months and Islamic history is remembered by such dates also.

[71] Bukharee no. 3935, Muslim 285

it was a Friday at the time of Zawwal (sun at its highest point). This area was the quarters of the tribe of Banee Saalim bin Awf. He ﷺ led the believers in the Friday prayer there at a valley called Ranwaan.

This was the first Friday prayer in Madinah to be given and the first ever Friday to be practiced in history of Al Islam. They were not able to offer this in Makkah due to the difficulties the idol worshipped forced upon them, no sermon was given or reminder preached and Allah knows best.[72]

ثُمَّ بَنَى الْمَسْجِدَ فِي قُبَاءِ   وَمَسْجِدَ الْمَدِينَةِ الْغَرَّاءِ

It was built the mosque of Qubaa

a famous place of worship like no other

ثُمَّ بَنَى الْمَسْجِدَ - This masjid is Al Qubaa, it is well known.

فِي قُبَاءِ - A famous area which is approximately six kilometers south of Masjid Al Nabawee. The building of Al Qubaa mosque was the first project he ﷺ worked on upon his arrival. It is situated near the area of Banee Umar Bin Awf. Here is a proof of the obligation to have a prayer facility in a Muslim area which is a priority of the community.

Ibn Katheer elaborates in his brilliant work '*Bidayah wal Nihayah*'[73] 'When the Prophet ﷺ entered Madinah riding the first place he stopped at was the district which Banee Umar ibn Awf lived, Al Qubaa. Some

[72] Bidaayah wal Nihaayah (526/4)
[73] (516/4)

people said he stayed twenty-two nights while others mention eighteen nights and it was also argued ten nights. Musaa Ibn Uqbah relayed that they camped there for three nights. But the most accurate account of this event was what has been recorded by Ibn Is'haq and others a duration between Monday to Friday. All of these time scales have been established concerning the building of masjid Al Qubaa. A virtuous mosque Allah praises with His magnificent verse:

﴿لَّمَسْجِدٌ أُسِّسَ عَلَى التَّقْوَىٰ مِنْ أَوَّلِ يَوْمٍ أَحَقُّ أَن تَقُومَ فِيهِ ۚ فِيهِ رِجَالٌ يُحِبُّونَ أَن يَتَطَهَّرُوا ۚ وَاللَّهُ يُحِبُّ الْمُطَّهِّرِينَ﴾

{A mosque founded on righteousness from the first day, is more worthy for you to stand in. within it are men who love to purify themselves; and allah loves those who purify themselves} (Al Tawbah: 108)

This verse is often repeated in the commentary [74] and supplementing this is also the hadith found in Sahih Muslim[75] about this masjid in Madinah and those who attend it.

وَمَسْجِدَ الْمَدِينَةِ الْغَرَّاء - The prayer place was built by the Prophet ﷺ. He first purchased the area surrounded by date palms owned by Suhail and Sahl who were two young orphans under the care of As'ad bin Zaraarah (May Allah be pleased with him). The masjid was built where the blessed camel of the Prophet sat down as described in Sahih Bukharee[76]. She assisted the people by providing milk and was used to help with the act of building. They chanted: *O' Allah indeed this is for the reward of the hereafter. Have mercy upon the Ansaar and the Muhajiroon'.*

---

[74] (212-216/4)
[75] No. 1398
[76] No.3932

ثُمَّ بَنَى مِنْ حَوْلِهِ مَسَاكِنَهْ   ثُمَّ أَتَى مِنْ بَعْدُ فِي هَذِي السَّنَةْ

Then he built her place close by

later that year, they then arrived

أَقَلُّ مِنْ نِصْفِ الَّذِينَ سَافَرُوا   إِلَى بِلاَدِ الْحُبْشِ حِينَ هَاجَرُوا

Fewer than half they travelled by fate

again to Abyssinia they did migrate

ثُمَّ بَنَى - He ﷺ built a place to live for his close ones (wives) which was a part or an extention of the mosque.

مَسَاكِنَهْ - He constructed a living quarter for Sawdah (May Allah be pleased with her) and then a final living space for Aishah (May Allah have mercy on her) that was adjacent to the prayer place (masjid).

Imam Al Dhahabi (Rahimullah) said 'It never reached us that nine buildings were erected alongside the masjid nor did we think this to be the case. He ﷺ wanted one apartment (room) for the mother of the believers Sawdah and did not require any other house until a house for Aishaa was built. Her chamber (Aishah) was complete in the month of Shawwal in the 2nd year of the hijrah. The Prophet built these places at different times'.[77]

[77] It is recorded in 'Bilbil Al Rawdh' (short abridged version of Al rawdhat Al Anf) and in 'Subul Al Hudaa wal Rashaad' (506/3) (56/13)

The apartments made where very modest and humble which are described in '*Adab Al Mufrad*' of Imam Al Bukharee[78] On the authority of Daawood ibn Qais "I saw that the rooms were made from the stumps of palm trees covered on the outside with smoothed hair. I think that the width of the house from the door of the room to the door of the house was about six or seven spans. The width of the room inside was ten spans. I think that the ceiling was between seven and eight, or there about."

ثُمَّ أَتَى مِنْ بَعْدُ فِي هَذِي السَّنَة - The rest of the migrants arrived.

أَقَلُّ مِنْ نِصْفِ الَّذِينَ سَافَرُوا - They were fewer than half in number compared to those that migrated to Abyssinia the second time. There were approximately eighty men and eighteen women. Al Saalihee writes in '*Subul Al Huda*'[79] 'While the believers were secure in Abyssinia under the rulership of Najashi, Abdullah Ibn Masood retreated back to Makkah and heard that the believers had migrated to Madinah ﷺ They then followed with thirty-three men and eight women.

The thirty-three men and eight women that travelled to Madinah shows us that the amount was less than half of those who migrated to Abyssinia the second time.

[78] No. 451, Shaykh Al Albanee classified authentic in the tahqeeq of 'Al Saheeh Adab Al Mufrad' (352)
[79] (524/2)

وَفِيهِ آخَى أَشْرَفُ الأَخْيَارِ   بَيْنَ الْمُهَاجِرِينَ وَالأَنْصَارِ

Paired them he did the noblest by far

between the Muhajireen and the Ansaar

وَفِيهِ - In the first of the hijrah.

آخَى أَشْرَفُ الأَخْيَارِ - He ﷺ (paired the the Muhajireen with the Ansaar).

Translator's note[80]

بَيْنَ الْمُهَاجِرِينَ وَالأَنْصَار - Those who migrated with him (Muhajiroon) were considered strangers in the community. Some had to split from their families and their dependents while others were tortured (i.e due to the message).

Ibn Al Qayyim (Rahimullah) explains in *'Zaad Al Maad'*[81] "The Messenger of Allah ﷺ paired between the two groups in the place of Anas ibn Malik and there were ninety men half were from the muhajireen and half were from the Ansaar. They were paired with one another and inherited from each other after death. They had more right over the bond of their own blood relatives until the time of Badr when the verse of Allah corrected their ways:

[80] The Muhajireen are those Muslims that migrated from Makkah and the Ansaar were the helpers from Al Madinah.
[81] (63/3)

﴿وَأُولُو الْأَرْحَامِ بَعْضُهُمْ أَوْلَىٰ بِبَعْضٍ فِي كِتَابِ اللَّهِ مِنَ الْمُؤْمِنِينَ وَالْمُهَاجِرِينَ﴾

{And those of (blood) relationship are more entitled (to inheritance) in the decree of Allah than (the other) the believers and the emigrants} (Surah Ahzaab: 6)

This verse of abrogation restored the inheritance of family over the ties of brotherhood.

From this brotherhood the Ansaar set a great example towards their brethren and Allah [The Most High] praised their kindness and hospitality:

﴿وَالَّذِينَ تَبَوَّءُوا الدَّارَ وَالْإِيمَانَ مِنْ قَبْلِهِمْ يُحِبُّونَ مَنْ هَاجَرَ إِلَيْهِمْ وَلَا يَجِدُونَ فِي صُدُورِهِمْ حَاجَةً مِمَّا أُوتُوا وَيُؤْثِرُونَ عَلَىٰ أَنْفُسِهِمْ وَلَوْ كَانَ بِهِمْ خَصَاصَةٌ ۚ وَمَنْ يُوقَ شُحَّ نَفْسِهِ فَأُولَٰئِكَ هُمُ الْمُفْلِحُونَ﴾

{And (also for) those who were settled in the home [i.e. Al-Madinah] and [adopted] the faith before them. They love those who emigrated to them and find not any want in their breasts of what they [i.e. the emigrants] were given but give [them] preference over themselves, even though they are in privation. And whoever is protected from the stinginess of his soul - it is those who will be the successful} (Al Hashr: 9)

This hospitality stretched to the extent that a man from amongst the Ansaar shared half of his wealth with a migrant that was paired with him by the Prophet ﷺ. Imam Al Bukharee also collected a hadith connected with this chapter of brotherhood.[82]

[82] No. 3937 / 5072

Narrated Anas (May Allah be pleased with him) said

'When Abdur-Rahman bin Auf came to Madinah and the Prophet ﷺ established the bond of brotherhood between him and Sa'd bin Ar-Rabi-al-Ansari, Sa'd suggestedAbdur-Rahman should accept half of his property and family. Abdur Rahman said "May Allah bless you in your family and property but guide me to the market." So Abdur-Rahman (while doing business in the market) made some profit from some condensed dry yoghurt and butter. After a few days the Prophet ﷺ saw him wearing clothes stained with yellow perfume. The Prophet ﷺ asked, "What is this, O `Abdur-Rahman?" He said, "O Allah's Messenger! I have married an Ansaari woman." The Prophet ﷺ asked, "What have you given her as dowry?" He (i.e. Abdur-Rahman) said, "A piece of gold, about the weight of a date stone." Then the Prophet said, "Give a banquet, even with one sheep."'

ثُمَّ بَنَى بِابْنَةِ[83] خَيرِ صَحْبِهِ   وَشَرَعَ الأَذَانَ فَاقْتَدِي[84] بِهِ
Built her place, his best friend's daughter
then explained the athan times as was ordered

ثُمَّ بَنَى - The Prophet ﷺ built a quarter for his wife Aishaa in the first year of the hijrah but it is said by the author and the people of knowledge it was performed in the 2nd year.

[83] With a ت would specify the female gender (of child).

[84] Other versions contain a ي for the assistance of the poetry's flow.

بَنَى بِابْنَةِ - This was for Aishah[85], the daughter of his closest companion.

خَيْرِ صَحْبِهِ - Abu Bakr Al Sideeq (May Allah be pleased with him).

Narrated Aisha[86]

The Prophet ﷺ engaged me when I was a girl of six (years). We went to Medina and stayed at the home of Bani-al-Harith bin Khazraj. Then I got ill and my hair fell out. Later on my hair grew (again) and my mother, Um Ruman came to me while I was playing on a swing with some of my friends. She called me and I went to her not knowing what she wanted to do to me. She took me by the hand and made me stand at the door of the house. I became breathless and when my breathing became all right she took some water and rubbed my face and head with it. Then she took me into the house. There in the house I saw some Ansari women who said, "Best wishes and Allah's Blessing and a good luck." Then she entrusted me to them and they prepared me (for the marriage). Unexpectedly Allah's Apostle came to me in the forenoon and my mother handed me over to him, at that time I was a girl of nine years of age.

Translator's note[87]

وَشَرَعَ الأَذَانَ - The order of the athan was instructed for the prayer. This happened because the command of the prayer was sent down without

[85] See Fat'h Al Baari of ibn Hajr (224/7)

[86] Sahih al-Bukhari 3894

[87] For some curious about the age difference between the Prophet and his wife Aishaa please refer to Robert Epstein's 'Teen 2.0 – Adolescence and Adultness'.

any fixed times. They would be told that the time of prayer was near and people would hasten to the masjid as recorded in the Sahihayn[88].

Ibn Umar narrates 'The believers reached Madinah and gathered together waiting for the prayer to be announced. One day they suggested a bell to be rung just like that of the Christians, others disagreed with this idea and suggested a trumpet similar to what the Jews have. Umar said "do we not have men that can proclaim the call to prayer?" The Prophet ﷺ then said "O' Bilal, stand up and call to the prayer"'.

This is not to be understood as the traditional call to prayer but it was one which "As Saalatul Jaam'ah" was shouted and the people would gather as written in the '*Tabaqaat' of Ibn Sa'd.*[89] Urwaa Bin Zubayr, Zaid Ibn Aslam and Saeed ibn Musayyib said 'Prior to the athaan the people in the time of the Messenger of Allah ﷺ were legislated to shout out "As Salaatul Jaam'aah" and the listeners responded.

Later on it was reported that Abdullah ibn Zaid had a dream hearing the words of the call to the prayer 'Allahu Akbar, Allahu Akbar...' until the end of the athan. After the Prophet ﷺ was informed he told him "Your dream was true God willing wake Bilal and teach him these words and let him make this call as he has a more appealing voice than you".

فَاقْتَدِ بِهِ - He is the Imam of the righteous and the ultimate example for the believers. He is the explainer of rights for the Muslims and followed the mua'thin in his words. He ﷺ used to reply to the words of his 'Come to Prayer, come to Success' by saying 'There is neither might nor power

[88] Al Bukharee no.604 Muslim 377
[89] (246/1)

except with Allah'. This is what has been transmitted regarding the Messenger of Allah.[90]

وَغَزْوَةُ الْأَبْوَاءِ بَعْدُ فِي صَفَرْ   هَذَا وَفِي الثَّانِيَةِ الْغَزْوُ اشْتَهَرْ

In Safar, Abwaa'aa shown

the second year hijri, a battle well known

إِلَى بُوَاطَ ثُمَّ بَدْرٍ وَوَجَبْ   تَحَوُّلُ الْقِبْلَةِ فِي نِصْفِ رَجَبْ

To Bawaat then Badr arranged

In the middle of Rajab the qiblah changed

مِنْ بَعْدِ ذَا الْعُشَيْرُ يَا إِخْوَانِي   وَفَرْضُ شَهْرِ الصَّوْمِ فِي شَعْبَانِ

Oh my brothers after ten days passing

in Sha'ban came the order of fasting

Here begin the battles from the life of Allah's Apostle ﷺ. These battles are worth explaining due to its great importance in his biography as well as the multiple benefits found within them. Al Khateeb Al Baghdadee (Rahimullah) reported in his work '*Al Jaamiah Al Ikhlaaq Al Raawi*'[91] on the narration of Isma'eel ibn Muhammad ibn Sa'd ibn Abi Waqqas Al Zuhri Al Madanee who said 'Our father used to teach us the battles of

[90] Bukharee 613
[91] No. 1590

the Messenger of Allah ﷺ and prepare us for it and its delegations'. He said "Oh my son, this is what moulded your forefathers so do not abandon it (its knowledge)".

It was also reported by [92] Zayd Al Abideen ibn Hussain ibn Ali that he said "*we used to know the battles of the Messenger of Allah ﷺ and its delegations just like we would know a surah from the Quran*". There were numerous battles the Prophet ﷺ actively engaged in and there were others that he did not take part in.

The Shaykh reported from Abu Is'haq Al Subay'ee who narrates I said to Zayd ibn Arqam (May Allah be pleased with him) "How many battles were there of the Messenger of Allah?" He replied "Nineteen", I asked "how many battles did you participate in with him?" he said "Seventeen battles"'.[93]

Al Haafidh ibn Hajr (Rahimullah) explained this narration of the wording "nineteen" meant the Prophet ﷺ went out into these battle whether he fought or not. The other narration of Abu Ya'laa is the same as Abi Zubayr from Jaabir who mentioned that the number of battles that occurred were twenty-one. This chain is authentic and its origin is from the collection of Imam Muslim. This alludes to the possibility that Zaid ibn Arqam did not recall two of them or counted two battles as one. Ibn Sa'd further elaborates on this matter by stating that there were seventeen battles the Prophet ﷺ was involved in.

[92] 1591

[93] Saheeh Bukharee no. 3949, Muslim 1254, in the last part of this 'Which one of them was first, he said 'The most difficult or the companion?'

Al Waqidee also held this stance and did not single out the battle of Waadi Quraa with Khaybar. As for the groups and delegations Ibn Is'haq counted thirty-six and Al Waqidee mentions forty-eight.

Other scholars such as Ibn Jawzee count fifty-two campaigns in his book '*At Talqeeh*' and Al Mas'oudy says sixty. Our Shaykh taught in his book '*Nadhm Al Seerah*' that the battles were more than seventy. Al Haakim expresses that there were more than one hundred battles as described in his work '*Al Ikleel*' and there have been scholars who suggested more than this.[94]

وَغَزْوَةُ الْأَبْوَاءِ بَعْدُ فِي صَفَرْ - The battle of Abwaa'ah took place in the 2nd year of the hijrah in the month of Safar. It was also named 'Waddan' which are two valley's located adjacent to each other just outside the city of Madinah by approximately twenty-four miles. There was no fighting in this battle however there was reconciliation between Bani Dhamrah bin Abdul Al Manaat Bin Kinaanah and their leader Majdy ibn Amr.

هَذَا وَفِي الثَّانِيَةِ الْغَزْوُ اشْتَهَر - The believers at this time had formed authority and reinforcements ready for combat that approached them and were ordered to fight. This was the start of a tremendous account in the 2nd year of the hijrah of the Prophet ﷺ.

إِلَى بُوَاط - The Prophet ﷺ next battled during Rabee Al Aakhir to 'Al Bawaat'. The believers wanted to stop and blockade the business caravans of the Quraysh when they reached Al Bawaat on the route of Radhwaa[95]. They retreated back to Madinah and did not find any of their

[94] Fat'h Al Baari (280-281/7)

[95] Al Haafidh said Al Murja' As Saabiq: A fat'ha pronunciation mark on the ر and a sukoon on some of the silent letters defines it as a great mountain in Yanbu.

plots or trickery so they prolonged the journey through Rabee Al Aakhir and part Jumad Al Awlaa.

ثُمَّ بَدْرٍ - Next occured the battle of Badr which took place in the month of Jumaad Al Akhir, it was also named the battle of Safwaan[96]. Kurz Ibn Jabir Al Fihree raided Madinah and the Prophet ﷺ ordered a group of men to chase them until they reached the valley of Safwaan which stood in the area of Badr. Kurz Ibn Jabir realised that they were not prepared to fight the Prophet ﷺ so he and his men fled, the dispatchment then returned to Madinah.

وَوَجَبْ تَحَوُّلُ الْقِبْلَةِ فِي نِصْفِ رَجَبْ - It was never differed between the people of knowledge that the qiblah changed from Bayt Al Maqdis (Al Aqsaa) to the sacred Ka'bah in the 2nd year of the hijrah. It changed direction before the great battle of Badr however the month it took place was debated. Some argued during Sha'ban while others said Jumaad Al Akhir.

The last opinion was Rajab and this was the author's stance (Rahimullah) along with the majority view. Al Hafidh ibn Hajr said in his book '*Al Fat'h*'[97] "The change of direction to prayer was done in the middle of Rajab in the 2nd year of the hijrah and that was the authentically established opinion of the majority has reported. This links back to Imam Al Haakim with an authentic chain from Ibn Abbas (May Allah be pleased with him).

[96] Al Hafidh said in the same reference (variations of some pronunciations)
[97] Al Fat'h (122/1) See 'Bidayah wal Nihayah (45/5)

مِنْ بَعْدِ ذَا الْعُشَيْرِ - The first incident of Badr was after the battle of Dhi Usheer also known as Al Usheerah or Al Usheeraa' by ten days[98]. The Prophet ﷺ went out by himself during Jumaad Al Awlaa until he reached an area in the middle of Yanbu and stayed there a month and a few nights during Jumaad Al Aakhir. Later he reconciled making a pact with the tribe of Banee Mudlij who were there. He retreated back to Madeenah and did not find any of the enemy's plots to harm him.

وَفَرْضُ شَهْرِ الصَّوْمِ فِي شَعْبَان - Fasting was mandated in Sha'baan in the 2nd year of the hijrah after the qiblah was redirected towards the Ka'bah by a month.[99]

وَالْغَزْوَةُ الْكُبْرَى الَّتِي بِبَدْرِ   فِي الصَّوْمِ فِي سَابِعِ عَشْرِ الشَّهْرِ

At the Badr this great battle vast

on the seventeenth day of the Ramadan fast

وَالْغَزْوَةُ الْكُبْرَى الَّتِي بِبَدْرِ - The first major battle began between the Muslims and the non believing tribe of Quraysh. The Quraysh proceeded forward with their caravans and wealth from Shaam lead by Abi Sufyaan who summoned them in Makkah to send reinforcements preparing them for battle.

The Prophet ﷺ came forth with his dispatchment until both parties got closer. They met the Muslimeen in an area called Badr which was well

[98] See: Al Fusool by Ibn Katheer (88)
[99] See: Al Bidayah wa Nihayah (52/5)

known and there was fighting in this battle. The muslims assembled their lines and by the persmission of Allah were granted victory and annihilation over the disbelievers.

The muslims captured some of them and killed another group, those whom were caught totalled seventy in number and those whom were killed equalled the same amount. The nobles and their chiefs were killed in this battle and in the night of this battle the Prophet ﷺ named the place that they would be buried[100].

Translators note[101]

He specifically assigned a part of the area to different people saying this area is for so and so and this area is for so and so. There were sheep belonging to the disbelievers that were captured in this battle and were many in quantity. This was the day which was named 'The day of the Criterion' in which Allah had titled in the Quran because this battle seperated truth and falsehood. A day the believers were given honour and humiliation dawned over the disbelieving folk. Ambassadors and authorities emerged representing Al Islaam setting horror into the hearts of the enemies and opponents.

فِي الصَّوْمِ فِي سَابِعِ عَشْرِ الشَّهْرِ - A historical milestone set in place on the seventeenth night of fasting in the blessed month of Ramadan in the 2nd year of the migration.

---

[100] Sahih Muslim no. 1779

[101] Here the Muslims fought in defence of the Qurayshi army that had various attempts to kill Allah's apostle. The final option for the believers was to fight that those that wanted to kill them, drive them out of their homes, broke peace agreements and did not want to co-exist. Never were the boundaries exceeded nor was injustice done to those that fought the Muslims. In fact, the Muslims obeyed the commands of warefare and did not transgress the limits of battle. The Quran taught the rights of how to deal with the captive and that if they surrender you submit alike.

وَوَجَبَتْ فِيهِ زَكَاةُ الْفِطْرِ　　مِنْ بَعْدِ بَدْرٍ بِلَيَالٍ عَشْرِ

Next was Zakah al Fitr as commanded

ten nights after the Badr standard

وَفِي زَكَاةِ الْمَالِ خُلْفٌ فَادْرِ　　وَمَاتَتِ ابْنَةُ النَّبِيِّ الْبَرِّ

Zakat Al Maal they differed to agree

then the passing of his child upon piety

وَوَجَبَتْ فِيهِ زَكَاةُ الْفِطْرِ - In the month of fasting Zakat Al Fitr was commanded.

زَكَاةُ الْفِطْرِ - The Zakat Al Fitr (Alms) in the month of Ramadan which a Saa' (two hand fulls) of food was distributed for the young, old, male, female, free and the enslaved. This is called Zakat Al Fitr because it represents the essence and spirit of giving from the month of Ramadan.

مِنْ بَعْدِ بَدْرٍ بِلَيَالٍ عَشْر - Zakat Al Fitr was obligated at the end of Ramadan ten nights after the battle of Badr. The battle commenced on the seventeeth night, ten nights after the zakat was obligated. Specifically, this was two or three days before the ending of the month of Ramadan.

Ibn Jareer Al Tabaree (May Allah have mercy on him) explained that Zakat Al Fitr was mandated in the 2nd year of the migration. It was also stated that the Messenger of Allah ﷺ delivered a sermon a day or two before the day of Fitr and commanded them to pay the zakah.[102]

وَفِي زَكَاةِ الْمَالِ - Another obligation that was constituted (Zakat Al Maal).

خُلْفٌ - There is a disagreement when this was actually ordered, the majority of the people of knowledge have stated that this was during the 2nd year of the hijrah of the Prophet ﷺ. Al-Imam Ibn Katheer (Rahimullah) writes in his work '*Al Bidaayah Wal Nihayah*' 'This year is also recorded by more than one of the latter scholars that Zakat was mandated at this time'.[103]

فَادْر - And taught them about it.

وَمَاتَتِ ابْنَةُ النَّبِيِّ الْبَرِّ

...then his child died upon piety

رُقَيَّةٌ قَبْلَ رُجُوعِ السَّفْرِ زَوْجَةُ عُثْمَانَ وعُرْسُ الطُّهْرِ

Ruqaiyah it was before he returned to abide

a pure soul, Uthman's beautiful bride

[102] Tareekh Al Umam wal Mulook (17/2)
[103] Al Bidaayah wa Nihaayah (54/5)

فَاطِمَةٍ عَلَى عَلِيِّ الْقَدْرِ وَأَسْلَمَ الْعَبَّاسُ بَعْدَ الأَسْرِ

Fatimah to Ali, he was in awe

then Abbas embraced this prisoner of war

وَمَاتَتِ ابْنَةُ النَّبِيِّ الْبَرّ - The death of Ruqaiyah, the daughter of the Messenger of Allah ﷺ.

قَبْلَ رُجُوعِ السَّفْر - Before the Quraishi army that travelled to Madinah to fight returned back. When the battle ended the Messenger of Allah ﷺ set up a camp[104] for three days before his return ﷺ as was established in the Sahihayn[105]'. 'If he passed by a people, he would stay with them for three days before returning. He ﷺ would proceed on with the captives of war, the sheep and caravans from the battle of Badr to Al Madinah. He sent people to convery glad tidings of their victory'.

From them was Abdullah ibn Rawaha (RadhiyAllahu Anh) who was sent to the dignitaries of Madinah and Zaid ibn Haarithah (Radhallahu anh) who was sent to the regular communities. Usamah Ibn Zaid mentions 'the news reached us while we were burying Ruqaiyah (RadhiyAllahu Anhaa) that victory and success was granted over those who associated partners with Allah'.

[104] Al Hafidh says in 'Al Fat'h (181/3). With various of pronunciation markings on the word 'Al Ersa' refers to an open area without any barriers or buildings.
[105] Sahih Al Bukharee 3065 / Muslim 2875

زَوْجَةُ عُثْمَانَ - Uthmaan Ibn Affan (May Allah be pleased with him) was looking after her in Madinah because of the order the Prophet of Allah ﷺ gave him as she was very ill. The Prophet ﷺ left for the battle of Badr while his daughter was sick but he was promised a share of the cattle from the war booty from Al Badr.[106]

و - At the end of the battle of Badr.

عُرْسُ الطُّهْرِ - The pure noble woman Fatimah Bint Muhammad[107] got wedded (May Allah be pleased with her).

عَلَى عَلِيِّ الْقَدْرِ - To a man with a great status and station in Al Islam Ali Ibn Abi Taalib (May Allah be pleased with him) who was the cousin of the Messenger of Allah ﷺ.

It was witnessed that Ali became the husband of Fatimah after the battle of Badr and this is authenticated in the Sahihayn[108]. Narrated Ali "I got an old she-camel as my share from the booty and the Prophet ﷺ had given me another from Al- Khumus. When I intended to marry Fatimah (daughter of the Prophet), I arranged that a goldsmith from the tribe of Bani Qainuqa would accompany me in order to bring Idhkhir (a valuable type of scented grass) and then sell it to the goldsmiths and use its price for my marriage banquet".

وَأَسْلَمَ الْعَبَّاسُ - Abbas, the uncle of the Prophet ﷺ embraced Islam.

---

[106] See: Al Bidayah wal Nihayah (311/5)
[107] Her name here is replaced with the word pure (various pronunciation types)
[108] Sahih Bukharee 2089 / Muslim 1979

بَعْدَ الأَسْر - He was one of the captives of war from the battle of Badr. It is differed when Abbas accepted Islam. Some said that he accepted Islam after he was a war prisoner and this was the opinion of the author. Other opinions mentioned that he embraced Islam before this because he marched with the army of idol worshippers at this battle (he disliked) and his Islam was hidden as was collected by Imam Ahmad[109]. People recorded a saying from him regarding the Quraysh 'I was a Muslim prior this and they hated me'.

وَقَيْنُقَاعُ غَزْوُهُمْ فِي الْإِثْرِ بَعْدَ ضَحَاءِ يَوْمِ عِيدِ النَّحْرِ

The aftermath trailed the Qaynuqa invasion

then the sacrificial Eid celebration

وَقَيْنُقَاعُ غَزْوُهُمْ فِي الْإِثْر - The tribe of Banu Qaynuqa was one of three Jewish tribes that resided in Madinah. He ﷺ migrated to them as his advent was promised. The Messenger of Allah ﷺ made a pact between the believers and this tribe and contracted the agreement in writing. Banu Qaynuqa was the first tribe of the Jews to break the peace treaty and terminated its agreement so they were invaded by the Prophet ﷺ. This was the after effects of the Battle of Badr in the middle of the month of Shawaal, they were barricaded for fifteen days until the cresent of Dhil Qi'dah. Allah then cast into their hearts terror for such treachery and deceit.

[109] No. 3310

The Prophet ﷺ ordered that they be tied up and was going to order the killing of their combatants until there was an intercession by Abdullah ibn Ubai whohad declared he was a Muslim (but he was one of the hypocrites. Abdullah insisted the Prophet not to kill them because of their disloyalty and disregard so he ﷺ instructed them to leave Al Madinah (to keep the people safe from their evil plots).[110]

بَعْدَ ضَحَاءِ يَوْمِ عِيدِ النَّحْرِ - Later came the sacrifice in Dhil Hijjah for the blessed Eid, 2nd year of the migration. Ibn Al Atheer (Rahimullah) said 'The Prophet ﷺ sacrificed an animal in Al Madinah and the people came out to the opening prayer place, he sacrificed two sheep although some scholars state one.[111] This was the milestone for this great ritual.

وَغَزْوَةُ السَّوِيقِ ثُمَّ قَرْقَرَةْ وَالْغَزْوُ فِي الثَّالِثَةِ الْمُشْتَهِرَةْ

Saweeq and Qarqara then occurred

well known battles in the year of the third

وَغَزْوَةُ السَّوِيقِ - When Abu Sufyan returned with the disbelieving Quraysh from the terrible defeat at Badr he promised he would never wash his face again until he sought revenge. A battalion of one hundred knights was assembled to travel to Madinah in the direction of Najd. This route would storm Madinah from the east, there they stumbled upon an area where a tribe of Jews resided.

[110] See: Seerah Al Nabawiyyah of ibn Hishaam (808-811/1)
[111] Asad Al Ghabaah 29/1

This place was named 'Al Areedh' which is a well known valley and its name is still used today in the eastern part of the city (Al Madinah). They sat and met a man called Sallam Bin Mishkim from this tribe who they quenched their thirst with and were fed by engaging in conversation with the people there. A plot was conjured up on how the Muslims would be attacked.

When things got heated corruption started and a siege on the Muslims begun in spite of revenge. An Ansaari man and his gardener were killed and the news began to spread rapidly. The Prophet ﷺ came out with a group and assigned Abu Lubabah as a leader over the people of Madinah, this incident was named Qaraqarah Al Kedr.

The Muslims proceeded further yet they missed Abu Sufyaan who was on the Fareen route with his convoy throwing out extra provisions of grounded wheat, flour and barley on the trail to lighten their load. This was their plot for an easy getaway from the Prophet ﷺ and his companions. The believers found a lot of these ingredients wasted on the escape route hence the name of the battle was title 'Ghazwat Al Saweeq' or 'The battle of the Flour Campaign'[112].

ثُمَّ قَرْقَرَة - This battle of Qarqarah Al Kudr was named here 'The Battle of Qarqarah' the author preferred this title over 'The battle of Saweeq' even though they are used interchangeablely as was stated by Al Waaqidy and Ibn Sa'd. The first part of the battle used the name 'Saweeq' then later 'Qarqarah Al Kudr'. 'The 'Saweeq Battle' begun in Dhil Hijjah and Qarqarah was in Muharram.[113] The correct view on this issue is that both of these separate occasions were one battle. Ibn

[112] See: Seerah Al Nabawiyyah of ibn Hishaam (804-806/1)

[113] See Al Maghaazi by Al Waaqidy (181-182/1) Tabaqaat Al Kubraa by Ibn Sa'd 30-31/2)

Katheer (Rahimullah) said 'The battle of Saweeq' took place in Dhil Hijjah and this was also 'the battle of Al Qarqarah Al Kudr."[114]

وَالْغَزْو - These battles.

فِي الثَّالِثَةِ الْمُشْتَهِرَة - Taking place in the third year of the famous migration and many other indications of this brought forward by the author to prove the date.

فِي غَطَفَانَ وَبَنِي سُلَيْم   وَأُمُّ كُلْثُومَ ابْنَةُ الْكَرِيم

At Ghatfaan and the tribe of Saleem

Umm Kulthoom, the blessed child of Al Ameen

زَوَّجَ عُثْمَانَ بِهَا وَخَصَّهْ   ثُمَّ تَزَوَّجَ النَّبِيُّ حَفْصَةْ

She married Uthmaan specifically...

then the Prophet to Hafsah rightfully

[114] A Bidaayah wal Nihaayah (302/5)

وَزَيْنَبًا ثُمَّ غَزَا إِلَى أُحُدْ فِي شَهْرِ شَوَّالٍ وَحَمْراءِ الْأَسَدْ

Zaynab next then Uhud had

In Shawwal, hamratul Asad

فِي غَطَفَانَ - The battle of Ghatfaan is also referred to as the battle of Dhi Amr. The Messenger of Allah ﷺ travelled out to a place in the direction of Najd. This place is nearby a well-known area today that goes by the name Al Nakheel. It is outside Madinah in the Eastern direction by approximately one hundred and twenty kilometres. It was the 3rd year of the prophetic migration that he went on this journey. They travelled to this place and spent their entire time there, they later returned without engaging in battle there.[115]

وَبَنِي سُلَيْمِ - Next was the battle of Bani Saleem that begun some time after the Battle of Badr. When the Muslims retreated back to Al Madinah there was no war or attacks for seven nights until this battle started. They reached Banee Saleem's base which was their watering source known as 'Al Kudr'. The Prophet ﷺ resided there for three nights and then returned back to Al Madinah without fighting[116]. This happened in the 2nd year and not the 3rd.

[115] See: Al Seerah Al Nabaweeyah by Ibn Hishaam (907-808/1)
[116] Same as (804/1)

Translator's note [117]

وَأُمُّ كُلْثُومَ ابْنَةُ الْكَرِيمِ زَوَّجَ عُثْمَانَ بِهَا وَخَصَّهْ - The Messenger ﷺ here married his daughter Umm Kulthoom to Uthman Ibn Affan (May Allah be pleased with him). Uthman previously married her sister Ruqaiyah who passed away before this near the time of the battle of Badr as previously mentioned. By this virtue he was titled 'The one with the two lights' or Dhil Nurayn because nobody else in hstory married two daughters of a prophet. He was successful and held this unique blessing (May Allah be pleased with him).

ثُمَّ تَزَوَّجَ النَّبِيُّ حَفْصَةَ - In this verse Allah's Apostle ﷺ married the daughter of Umar Ibn Al Khattab (May Allah be pleased with him). Ibn Katheer highlights in '*Al Fusool*'[118] 'He ﷺ married Hafsah Bint Umar in the 3rd year of the hijrah'.

Bukharee narrates[119] on the authority of Abdullah ibn Umar (May Allah be pleased with him) who said:

'Umar bin Al-Khattab said "When Hafsa bint 'Umar became a widow after the death of (her husband) Khunais bin Hudhafa As-Sahmi who was a companion of the Prophet ﷺ. He died in Madinah and I approached Uthman bin 'Affan to suggest Hafsa (for marriage) to him. He said, "I will think it over." I waited for a few days until he met me and said, "It seems that it is not possible for me to marry at this present time". Umar added "I then met with Abu Bakr As-Siddique and said to

[117] This battle started because the Prophet of Allah heard that the tribe of Saleem were about to invade Madinah and the Muslims had to prevent it so they headed to the Jewish tribe's area before chaos erupted in Al Madinah.
[118] Page 230
[119] Saheehah 5122

him "If you wish, I will marry my daughter Hafsa to you"; Abu Bakr kept quiet and did not say anything to me in reply. I became angrier with him than I did with 'Uthman. I waited for a few more days and then Allah's Apostle asked for her hand and I gave her in marriage to him. Afterwards I returned to Abu Bakr who said "Perhaps you became angry with me when you presented Hafsa to me and I did not give you a reply?" I said, "Yes!" Abu Bakr replied "Nothing stopped me from responding to your offer except that I knew that Allah's Apostle had mentioned her concerning marriage and I never wanted to reveal the secret of the Prophet. If Allah's Apostle had refused her, I would have accepted her".

وَزَيْنَبًا - Later the Messenger of Allah ﷺ contracted a marriage agreement with Zaynab Bint Khuzaymah Al Halaaleyah. Ibn Is'haq states[120] 'The Prophet married Zaynab Bint Khuzaymah after Hafsah who was known as 'The mother of the poor'. Previously she was wedded to Husayn bin Harith or his brother Tufayl Bin Harith ibn Abdul Mutallib ibn Al Manaaf. She was the first woman to pass away in Madinah and she bore no children to him ﷺ.

ثُمَّ غَزَا إِلَى أُحُدْ فِي شَهْرِ شَوَّالٍ - In the 2nd year of the hijrah we find a great event when Allah [The Most High] trialed the believing people with a great test. This distinguished those who truly believed from those whom were plain hypocrites. This battle made apparent the true colours of the disbelievers of Islam which occurred after the battle of Badr. This conquest of Uhud that approched strengthened the believers' rows and seventy amongst them were martyred. The master of the martyrs Hamzah ibn Abdul Mutallib was killed and the Prophet was severly injured on his face. His lower right tooth was smashed out of his mouth

[120] As Seerah Al Nabaweeyah (281/1)

by a rock and his white hair was pulled out ﷺ. This day a tremendous verse from Al Quran was revealed unto them from the chapter Al Imraan:

﴿وَإِذْ غَدَوْتَ مِنْ أَهْلِكَ تُبَوِّئُ الْمُؤْمِنِينَ مَقَاعِدَ لِلْقِتَالِ ۗ وَاللَّهُ سَمِيعٌ عَلِيمٌ﴾

{And [remember] when you, [O Muhammad], left your family in the morning to post the believers at their stations for the battle [of Uhud] - and Allah is Hearing and Knowing} (Al Imran: 121)

From the wisdom and nature of Allah is that His messengers along with those that follow sometimes defeat and other times they are defeated to highlight the consequences of one's actions. If they were to always be victorious there will never be a distinction between those who are truly convicted and truthful from the others.

On the contrary if they are always defeated then the objective of the prophethood will never be achieved hence Allah has balanced these two matters in order to judge who will follow and obey the truth through victory and loss. This was the lesson learned at Uhud and that day the consequence struck the believers.[121]

Translator's note[122]

وَحَمْرَاءِ الأَسَد - After the battle of Uhud the Muslims experienced much grief and pain. The Messenger of Allah ﷺ was preparing the next move to retaliate the enemy so he did not allow anyone to proceed with him except that they were involved in the battle of Uhud. (The disbelieving folk were always on the prawl to defeat the Prophet and his army after

[121] See: Zaad Al Maad (219/3)

[122] Please refer to the battle of Uhud for more details of what took place and how the Muslims were defeated

they drove them out of their homes, tortued them severely leaving them to settle in Madinah. They did not want Islam to spread nor were willing to submit).

Jabir Ibn Abdullah (May Allah be pleased with him) commenced this invasion, his father was martyred at Uhud when leaving behind his family and daughters. He sought permission from the Prophet ﷺ to go out to Hamratul Asad and was granted permission. The believers also rose by the order of the Messenger of Allah ﷺ even though they were still exhausted and heavily wounded in their limbs. Hamratul Asad is an area twenty kilometers outside Madinah from the southern direction, with this Allah revealed a great reminder:

﴿الَّذِينَ اسْتَجَابُوا لِلَّهِ وَالرَّسُولِ مِنْ بَعْدِ مَا أَصَابَهُمُ الْقَرْحُ لِلَّذِينَ أَحْسَنُوا وَاتَّقَوْا مِنْهُمْ أَجْرٌ عَظِيمٌ﴾

{Those [believers] who responded to Allah and the Messenger after injury had struck them. For those who did well among them and feared Allah is a great reward} (Al Imraan: 172)[123]

فَالْخَمْرُ حُرِّمَتْ يَقِينًا فَاسْمَعَنْ هَذَا وَفِيهَا وُلِدَ السِّبْطُ الْحَسَنْ

Alcohol was forbidden they certainly heard

then Hassan was born in that very same year

الْخَمْرُ حُرِّمَتْ - Alcohol was forbidded in the 3rd year of the hijrah which was well known amongst the majority of the people of knowledge.

[123] See: Bidayah wal Nihayah (454/5) Al Fusool by Ibn Katheer (119-120)

Others have held that it was prevented in the 4th year following the battle of Bani Nadheer.

يَقِينًا - This legislation was an order that was evidently established with certainty. It was a prohibition finding no doubt concerning it. It was stopped when Allah [The Most Supreme] legislated:

﴿يَا أَيُّهَا الَّذِينَ آمَنُوا إِنَّمَا الْخَمْرُ وَالْمَيْسِرُ وَالْأَنْصَابُ وَالْأَزْلَامُ رِجْسٌ مِنْ عَمَلِ الشَّيْطَانِ فَاجْتَنِبُوهُ لَعَلَّكُمْ تُفْلِحُونَ﴾

{O you who have believed, indeed, intoxicants, gambling, [sacrificing on] stone alters [to other than Allah], and divining arrows are but defilement from the work of Satan, so avoid it that you may be successful}

(Al Maaidah: 90)

فَاسْمَعْنَ - They listened and obeyed without protest or opposition.

وَفِيهَا - In the 3rd year (of the migration).

وُلِدَ السِّبْطُ - The grandson of the Prophet was born, Al Hassan Ibn Ali Ibn Abi Talib (May Allah be pleased with him). Ibn Hajr (Rahimullah) describes in his work 'Al Isaabah' 'Hassan Ibn Ali ibn Abi Taalib ibn Abdul Mutallib Bin Hishaam Bin Abdul Manaaf Al Haashimi was the grandson of the Prophet ﷺ. He was his precious offspring, a leader of the believers, Abu Muhammad who was born in the middle of Ramadan in the 3rd year of the migration. Ibn Sa'd, Ibn Barqee and another scholar mentioned that he was born in Sha'baan, some argued in the 4th year and others said the 5th but the first position is well established'.

وَكَانَ فِي الرَّابِعَةِ الْغَزْوُ إِلَى بَنِي النَّضِيرِ فِي رَبِيعٍ أَوَّلا

In the fourth it was the battle to be

with the tribe of Nadheer in first of Rabee

وَكَانَ فِي الرَّابِعَة - An event occured in the 4th year after the Prophetic migration that followed the battle of Uhud. The author here takes the view of Ibn Is'haq[124] which Urwah ibn Zubayr and Al Zuhree recollect this battle taking place before the battle of Uhud.[125]

الْغَزْوُ إِلَى بَنِي النَّضِير - An invasion of the Jewish tribe Banee Nadheer.

فِي رَبِيعٍ أَوَّلا - During Rabee Al Awwal. The reason this expedition happened was because a man from among the companions of the Prophet ﷺ killed two men who had a contractual agreement with the Prophet ﷺ which he didn't know about. When the Messenger of Allah ﷺ was informed of this injustice he said "There is a debt upon them both".

The Prophet went out with Abu Bakr, Umar and a man from the tribe of Bani Nadheer to pay the blood money for the two victims. He sat amongst them to arrange the affair. Their interests were secretive planning to kill him there as they whispered to one another "Whoever drops the boulder on Muhammad will kill him". This evil deed was to

[124] Seerah of Ibn Hishaam (993/2)
[125] See: Saheeh Al Bukharee with Fat'h Al Baari (330/7)

be carried out by Amro Bin Jahash (May the curse of Allah be upon him).

The angel Jibreel delivered the revelation to him from the Lord of the worlds that these men were plotting to kill him, upon hearing this he ﷺ quickly retreated back to Madinah. Shortly after he prepared his men for the battle against Banee Nadheer due to the breaking the oath they had with the Prophet ﷺ with the gravest betrayals to assassinate him.

Translator's note[126]

Allah's Apostle ﷺ and his army marched forth and surrounded them for six nights and Allah cast terror in the enemies' hearts . Banee Nadheer requested the Messenger ﷺ to leave them alone and stop fighting as they will give up everything they owned what they carried on their camels except for their weaponary and he accepted their request. For them Allah revealed a verse from the chapter of Al Hashr.[127]

وبَعْدُ مَوْتُ زَيْنَبَ الْمُقَدَّمَةْ   وَبَعْدَهُ نِكَاحُ أُمِّ سَلَمَةْ

The death of Zaynab was surely close by

Umm Salamah's nikkah was next in line

وبَعْدُ – After the previous event.

[126] It was the companion Amr Bin Umayyah that wanted to avenge the death of his friend's following the Ma'oonah massacre so killed two of them during their sleep. The Prophet was extremely saddened by this tragedy.

[127] See: Al Seerah ibn Hishaam (793-797/2) Bidayah wal Nihayah (533-549/5)

مَوْتُ زَيْنَبَ - Zaynab Al Khuzayma A Halaaleyah, Umm Al Masakeen, the Prophet ﷺ wife.

الْمُقَدَّمَةْ – The author mentioned the marriage of the Prophet was close by ﷺ. Al Hafidh states in '*Al Isaabah*'[128] 'The Prophet ﷺ consummated his marriage with Zaynab after he had consummated with Hafsah Bint Umar. He did not abide with her except for two or three months until she passed away (RadhiyAllahu Anhaa). Al Kalby collected that he ﷺ married her in the month of Ramadan in the 3rd year and he lived with her for eight months in which she died in the 4th year of Rabee Al Aakhir.

وَبَعْدَهُ نِكَاحُ أُمِّ سَلَمة - Bint Amiah Bin Al Mughirah Al Qurayshi Al Makhzumiyah. When this woman accepted Islam long ago she was wedded to Abu Salma Bin Abdul Asad ibn Al Mughirah. She migrated to Abysinnia and gave birth to Salma before returning back to Makkah. She finally moved to Madinah to live amongst the believers. Her husband firstly migrated then she followed him and when he passed away she married the Messenger of Allah ﷺ.

It is reported in Sahih Muslim [129]on the authority of Umm Salma (May Allah be pleased with her) that she said: I heard the Messenger of Allah ﷺ say:

"No Muslim is afflicted with a calamity but that he should say what Allah has commanded him. ***Indeed, to Allah we belong and to Allah we will return. O Allah reward me in my affliction and replace it with something***

[128] (426-427/13)
[129] No. 918

better than it. *If he does so, Allah will replace it with something better than it."*

Translators note[130]

When Abu Salma passed away she asked "Which Muslim is better than Abu Salma?" He was the first household to migrate to the Messenger of Allah ﷺ which I read the dua, Allah then replaced him with the Messenger of Allah for me to marry ﷺ. The Messenger of Allah requested Hatib ibn Balta (May Allah be pleased with him) to marry me to him. I informed him 'Indeed I have a daughter and I am very jealous woman' in which he replied "Concerning your daughter I ask Allah to enrich her and I pray to Allah to depart you from your envious ways".

After the passing of Zaynab, Ibn Hajr narrates in '*Al Isaabah*'[131] that Ibn Sa'd explained the event of Umm Salama which has a broken chain regarding the Prophet's engagement to her. She said 'The Prophet married me and transferred me to Zaynab Bint Khuzayma's house after she departed this world'.

وَبِنْتِ جَحْشٍ ثُمَّ بَدْرِ الْمَوْعِدِ[132] وَبَعْدَهَا الْأَحْزَابُ فَاسْمَعْ وَاعْدُدِ

The daughter of Jahsh with Badr's account

and hearing the enemies in their enormous amount

[130] This was revealed as a verse from the Quran also (156/2)
[131] (427/13)
[132] A promise

وَبِنْتِ جَحْشٍ - The Prophet ﷺ married Zaynab Bint Jahsh Al Asadeeyah in the 4th year after his prophetic migration, the author and others held this same view. It was also believed they wedded in the 3rd year and in the 5th by another party of scholars.[133]

The verse regarding Al Hijaab was revealed due to her specific circumstance. Prior to this she was under the care and protection of Zaid ibn Harithah (as her mahram) so the verse was revealed regarding her:

﴿فَلَمَّا قَضَىٰ زَيْدٌ مِنْهَا وَطَرًا زَوَّجْنَاكَهَا لِكَيْ لَا يَكُونَ عَلَى الْمُؤْمِنِينَ حَرَجٌ فِي أَزْوَاجِ أَدْعِيَائِهِمْ إِذَا قَضَوْا مِنْهُنَّ وَطَرًا وَكَانَ أَمْرُ اللَّهِ مَفْعُولًا﴾

{... So when Zayd had no longer any need for her, we married her to you in order that there not be upon the believers any discomfort concerning the wives of their adopted sons when they no longer have need of them. And ever is the command of Allah accomplished} (Al Ahzaab: 37)

She was married by the decree of the Lord and also collected in the narration of Bukharee[134]

On the Authority of 'Aishah (May Allah be pleased with her) the Messenger of Allah ﷺ said "the one who will die after me is the one with the longest arm"; she said that Zaynab had the longest arm amongst (metaphorically) as she used to help the poor frequently and give plenty of charity.

[133] See Al Isaabah (417/13) Subul Al Hudaa wal Rashaad fi Seerah khayr al Ibaad (108/12)
[134] No. 7420

ثُمَّ بَدْرِ الْمَوْعِدِ - At last the appointed battle of Badr or also known as 'The Final Badr' approached them. There are three battles that are connected to the battle of Badr – the First Badr, The Great and The Final. This final Badr also adopted the name the appointed Badr because it was an appointment for the believers after their defeat at Uhud.

The Prophet ﷺ set out to a specific place and camped there for eight nights until the disbelievers of the Quraysh arrived from Makkah under the leadership of Abi Sufyaan. They reached Majannah from the direction of Dhahran and started preparing to return (out of cowardice).

Abu Sufyan proclaimed 'O People of the Quraysh! Nothing will improve your condition except a fruitful year, where you eat from your vegetation and drink from your milk and this will be a very dry rainless year so I am returning, return back with me'[135]

وَبَعْدَهَا - After the battle of the appointed Badr was the battle of the confederates or Al Ahzaab that was on the horizon also known as the battle of Al Khandaq or The Trenches. Ibn Katheer (Rahimullah) mentions in '*Al Fusool*'[136] 'Allah sent upon the believers a great test and shook them. He grounded their hearts with true faith and protection. This battle revealed the true hypocrites and it humiliated them with great shame. It ended with a great victory for the Muslims, His slave and the enemy was defeated. The All Mighty enriched His army with honour and left the disbelievers with rage and frustration because the Muslims

[135] Seerah Ibn Hishaam (1017/2) / Bidayah wa Nihayah (573-578/5)
[136] Page 135-136

overcame their evil cunning schemes. This was from the great bounty of their Lord.

They were prevented from attacking or fighting the believers from then on having finished completely helpless and the Muslims were victorious and all praise is due to Allah (Lord of all that exists). According to the historians of the events of warfare and the scholars of the seerah this took place in the 5th year of the hijrah in the month of Shawaal'. This turn of event was also authenticated by Ibn Al Qayyim (Rahimullah) and others.[137]

The great scholars of Al Islam wrote that this battle dated back to the 4th year of the hijrah. Great teachers including Musaa ibn Uqbah and Ibn Hazm both described that there was '*no doubt*' regarding the time of this battle. An opinion the author believed in but also wanted to point out the differences between the shuyookh concerning it.

The reason for the battle of Al Khandaq commencing was that a party from amongst the Jews of Banee Nadheer (who were expelled from Madinah and Al Khaybar) set out with the Quraysh from Makkah to plan an unholy attack upon the Messenger of Allah ﷺ. They promised themselves victory after their cowardice at Badr so they proceeded forward.

This coup from Banee Nadheer travelled a journey to the tribe of Ghatfaan and called out its inhabitants for reinforcements which they responded to in the affirmative. Abu Sufyan ibn Harb led his men and cavalry whilst Uyaynah ibn Hisn led his. Both delegations combined had approximately ten thousand soldiers. When the news reached the Messenger of Allah ﷺ he ordered the Muslims (by the idea of Salman Al Farsi – (May Allah be pleased with him) to dig huge trenches around

[137] See Zaad Al Ma'aad (279/3)

the borders of Madinah as a buffer zone and a shield from the idol worshippers (i.e the enemy). The Muslims followed suit and dug perfect trenches. They were roughly three thousand in number as correctly recorded by the scholars of Al Madinah. They were also summoned to tie essentials to their backs. He ﷺ told the women and their offsprings to prepare the food whilst Ibn Umm Al Maktoom was responsible over them (May Allah be pleased with him).

The tribe of Banu Quraydha also broke their agreement between them and the Prophet ﷺ not to wage war upon each other. This was very dangerous and constituted high risk for the believers as they had been striken with a huge trial just before the battle. They knew this was a huge test as Allah revealed concerning their situation:

﴿هُنَالِكَ ابْتُلِيَ الْمُؤْمِنُونَ وَزُلْزِلُوا زِلْزَالًا شَدِيدًا﴾

{There the believers were tested and shaken with a severe shaking} (Al Ahzaab: 11)

Allah [The All-Mighty] then decreed a matter to fail within the ranks of the disbelieving enemy. Their strong unit was dismantled by a great windy storm which shook them tremendously with gusts and thunder for many nights.[138]

فَاسْمَعْ - (listen) Be attentive to this mighty news concerning the battles of the Prophet Muhammad ﷺ

وَاعْدُدِ – Take care of it by understanding these numbered events and its history.

[138] Al Fusool fi seerah Ibn Katheer (137-140) Abridged

ثُمَّ بَنِي قُرَيْظَةٍ وَفِيهِمَا خُلْفٌ وَفِي ذَاتِ الرِّقَاعِ عُلِمَا

The battle of Quraydha next behind

Dhaat Ar Riqaa they learned in time

كَيْفَ صَلَاةُ الْخَوْفِ وَالْقَصْرُ نُمِي وَآيَةُ الْحِجَابِ وَالتَّيَمُّمِ

The prayer of fear and to shorten right

and the verse of hijab and how to wipe

قِيلَ: وَرَجْمُهُ الْيَهُودِيَّيْنِ وَمَوْلِدُ السِّبْطِ الرِّضَا الْحُسَيْنِ

The Jewish couple were publicly punished

and the birth of Hussain pleasingly flourished

ثُمَّ - The next (battle)

بَنِي قُرَيْظَة - We understood that they had broken the pact and trust at the battle of Al Khandaq. They (Banu Quraydha) convinced the Quraysh to attack the Muslims in that particular battle. Once the Prophet ﷺ finished from the mission of Al Ahzaab he engaged in battle with them.

In the Sahihayn[139] Narrated 'Aishah 'When Allah's Apostle returned on the day (of the battle) of Al-Khandaq (i.e. Trench), he put down his arms and took a bath. Then Gabriel whose head was covered with dust came

[139] Bukharee no. 2713,4117,4122 Muslim no. 1769

to him saying, "You have put down your arms! By Allah, I have not put down my arms yet." Allah's Apostle said, "Where to now?" Gabriel said, "This way," pointing towards the tribe of Bani Quraydha. So Allah's Apostle went out towards them'.

Abdullah Ibn Umar narrated 'The Prophet ﷺ said to us on the return of Al Ahzab "*No one among you should pray Asr except at Banu Quraydha.*"[140] Some of us left out Asr during the travel and said "*we will not pray Asr until we reach our destination*" others said "*We will pray now*" and none of the groups were incorrect. When the Prophet ﷺ was informed of this differing, he did not rebuke anyone for their conclusion.

The Jewish tribes broke the peace agreements with the Prophet during the the great battles that took place between the Prophet of Islam ﷺ and the idol worshippers. Banu Qaynuqa broke the treaty after Al Badr, Banu Nadheer after Al Uhud and Banu Quraydha after Al Ahzaab.

وَفِيهِمَا خُلْفٌ - In historical texts these were two seperate battles, Al Ahzaab and Banu Quraydha yet scholars differed.

وَفِي ذَاتِ الرِّقَاعِ - There was a battle named Dhat Al Riqaa' in the direction of 'Najd' where Bani Maharib along with Bani Tha'labah from Ghatfaan were fought against. The reason for its name 'Dhat Al Riqaa' was because some[141] indicated that they (the Muslims) wrapped their legs and feet in cloth to protect them for the severe heat which would burn them and supports to this are found in the Sahihayn[142] From the

[140] Sahih Al Bukharee 947, 4119 with his wording. Muslim no. 1770 with the wording of 'Dhur'
[141] See: Bidayah wal Nihayah (559/5)
[142] Bukharee 4178 / Muslim 1816

narration of Abu Buraydah what has been transmitted on the authority of Abu Musa (Ash'ari) who said:

"We set out on an expedition with the Messenger of Allah ﷺ. We were six in number and had (with us) only one camel[113] which we rode in turns,[114] and our feet were injured. My feet were so badly injured that my nails dropped off. We covered our feet with rags hence this expedition was titled Dhat-ur-Riqa' (i. e. the expedition of rags) because we bandaged our feet with rags (on that day). Abu Burda said that Abu Musa narrated this tradition, and then disliked repeating it as he did not want to give any publicity to what he did in this noble cause and cause his deeds to be in vain."

A disagreement concerns the time this battle took place which Ibn Qayyim took the correct stance[115] as well as Ibn Katheer[116] who hold that it happened after the battle of the Trenches.Their reasonings for this was because Ibn Umar was given the permission to partake in the battle of Al Khandaq for the first time (the battle of the Trenches). It was established in the collection of Bukharee and Muslim[117].

He (May Allah be pleased with him) said "I fought alongside the Messenger of Allah ﷺ towards Najd (Dhaat Al Riqaa) and remembered the prayer of fear".

---

[113] Al Hafidh mentions in 'Al Fat'h' (421/7) We rode the camel in turns, one would mount then he would descend for the next person to ride until we reached their camp.
[114]Al Hafidh states in the previous citings with the fat'h on the noon and the kesra on the Qaaf to mean single turns. The camel was mounted on and it is said one rode the camel and the other walked until the camel's hoof became worn out.
[115] See: Zaad Al Maad (202-204/3)
[116] Al Fusool fi seeratil Rasool (130-131)
[117] Bukharee no. 4132, 4133 / Muslim 839

Translator's note[148]

عُلِمَ - The Prophet ﷺ (taught).

كَيْفَ صَلاَةُ الخَوْفِ - The Prophet ﷺ taught his companions how to establish the prayer of fear which was during this battle. Ibn Qayyim (Rahimullah) describes 'This stance was taken by Ibn Is'haq and the people who analysed the biography of the Prophet ﷺ and warfare in particular this battle. However, the opinion of praying this fear prayer is very problematic because the the idolators refrained the Prophet ﷺ from performing the Asr prayer on the day of Al Khandaq until the sun had set.

The clearest stance was that the first prayer of fear was (instructed) at Usfaan. This is in agreement with the hadith collected by Al Imam Tirmidhee that they prayed at Dhat Al Riqaa' which he was taught and performed after the invasion at Usfaan. There is no contention amongst scholars that the battle of Usfaan took place after the battle of the trench (Al Khandaq), Abu Hurayrah and Abu Musaa witnessed 'Dhat Al Riqaa'.[149]

وَالقَصْرُ - Shortening the prayers that consist of four units (rakah).

نُمِي - To lift the burdon off himself and make his affair easier. ﷺ It was documented to have taken place in the 4th year. Ibn Atheer said "the shortening of the prayers occurred in the 4th year"[150].

---

[148] If it is authentically established that Ibn Umar firstly battled at Al Khandaq, we must understand that the battles he mentions after this are post Al Khandaq or Al Ahzaab.
[149] Zaad Al Maad (202-205/3)
[150] Asad Al Ghabah (29/1)

وَآيَةُ الْحِجَابِ - Al Hafidh Ibn Katheer commentates in *Al Fusool*[151]

"There is no disagreement that the verse of Al hijab was revealed in the morning that followed the night he consummated his marriage with Zaynab Bint Jahsh. As for the precise time that this happened then there is a differing which will be pointed out.

Translator's note[152]

وَالتَّيَمُّم - The Quranic verse regarding purifying yourself for prayer (with natural earth if no water is available i.e. Tayammum) was revealed in this year also. The reason for this revelation was due to Aishah (May Allah be pleased with her) losing a necklace of hers in one of the battles in the 4th year and the view of the author (Rahimullah). Other scholars held the position that it was shortly after the battle of Banee Mustalaq.[153]

Translators note[154]

قِيلَ: وَرَجْمُهُ الْيَهُودِيَّيْنِ - A story was told where two jewish people were stoned by the Messenger of Allah ﷺ in the 4th year of the hijrah. Ibn

[151] Pg 107

[152] Narrated Anas bin Malik I of all the people know best this verse of Al-Hijab. When Allah's Apostle married Zainab bint Jahsh she was with him in the house and he prepared a meal and invited the people (to it). They sat down (after finishing their meal) and started chatting. So the Prophet went out and then returned several times while they were still sitting and talking. Allah revealed the Verse **'O you who believe! Enter not the Prophet's houses until leave is given to you for a meal, (and then) not (so early as) to wait for its preparation... ask them from behind a screen.' (33.53)** the screen was set up and the people went away. (Bukharee 6:60:315)

[153] See: Fat'h Al Baaree (432/1) and Zaad Al Ma'ad (257-259/3)

[154] The Muslim delegation was stranded for a while when the prayer time came in, Allah instructed them to make tayammum as no water was accessible.

Atheer [Rahimullah] mentions 'From the two that were ﷺ stoned was a man and a woman and this account is well-known'.[155]

And what was record by Al Bukharee and Muslim[156].

Narrated Ibn Umar

A Jewish man and Jewish woman were brought to Allah's Apostle ﷺ on a charge of committing illegal sexual intercourse. The Prophet asked them: "What is the legal punishment (for this sin) in your Book (Torah)?" They replied "Our rabbis have innovated the blackening of faces with charcoal and Tajbiya" (being mounted on a donkey, with their faces in opposite directions, and then mortified in public). Abdullah bin Salaam said "O Allah's Apostle tell them to bring the Torah". The Torah was brought forth and then one of the Jews covered the verse of the Rajm (stoning to death) with their hand. They started reading what preceded and what followed it. On that Ibn Salaam said to the Jew "Lift up your hand". The verse of the stoning was under his hand therefore Allah's Apostle ﷺ ordered that the two (sinners) be stoned to death, and so they were stoned."

Abdullah Ibn Umar said that "We were stoning the two Jewish people and I saw the man protecting the lady by guarding his body over hers".

Translator's note[157]

---

[155] Asad Al Ghabah (29/1) See: Imta' Al Isma' by Al Maqreezi (202/1)

[156] Bukharee no. (6841/2625) Muslim no. 1699 with his wording

[157] This form of corporal punishment acted as a deterrent for the people under the rule of the land in order to protect and preserve people. They were carried out on thieves, sexual assaulters, terrorists etc. These crimes were judged and weighed out before any penalty was implemented. This form of punishment served as a last option if the perpetrator continued to commit evil intentionally and publicly. The severity of the crime was also taken into account to judge its punishment. Bear in mind that these

وَمَوْلِدُ السِّبْطِ الرِّضَا الْحُسَيْنِ - In the 4th year of the prophetic hijrah. Al Haafidh ibn Hajr describes in '*Al Isaabah*'[158] "Hussayn Ibn Ali ibn Abi Taalib ibn Abdul Mutallib ibn Hishaam ibn Abdul Manaaf Al Hashimi, Abu Abdullah, the grandson of the Prophet ﷺ and his beloved.

Az Zubayr and others mention that 'He was born in the month of Sha'baan in the 4th year, some say in the 6th year and others say in the 7th but there is no harm served with any of the conclusions'. The closest report was that he was indeed born in the 4th year and this was also the position of the author [Rahimullah].

اَلْإِفْكُ فِي غَزْوِ بَنِي الْمُصْطَلِقِ وَكَانَ فِي الْخَامِسَةِ اسْمَعْ وَثِقِ

The incident of Al Ifk and the Mustaliq tribe

listen and trust in the year hijrah five

وَكَانَ فِي الْخَامِسَةِ اسْمَعْ وَثِقِ - In the 5th year we observe the incident of Al Ifk (the rumour) concerning the mother of the believers Aishah (May Allah be pleased with her). Allah revealed the glorious words freeing her from the evil slander that conspired against her to distort her reputation.

She modestly said "*I never thought that Allah would send down anything about my affair, divine inspiration that would be recited (forever), as I*

punishments are not to be taken out by anyone except the leading legitimate authority of the land under that constitution in a due process. The Jewish people lived under the shariah in safety and protection for generations; such punishments were set up for all people who transgressed against the law and not just Jewish folk. In this case of adultery, the stoning was instructed by that which was legislated in the Torah of the Jewish tradition at that time.

[158] (547/2)

considered myself too unworthy to be talked of by Allah with something that was to be recited"[159].

Ibn Katheer (Rahimullah) explains in his Tafseer[160] 'The scholars have collectively gathered that whomsoever curses or dishonours her after this and acuses her like the one who acused her in the verses (ayaat) then that person is an outright disbeliever because they have gone in opposition to the Quran.'

فِي غَزْوِ بَنِي الْمُصْطَلِقِ - In the 5th year of the hijrah the Prophet engaged in battle with Banee Mustalliq and the author added that some have held it was the 6th year.

بَنِي الْمُصْطَلِقِ - They are the leaders over Banu Khuza'ah, their grandfather was 'Al Mustallaq'. This battle was called 'Al Mureysi' due to the area where they lived was called 'Al Mureysi'. The Prophet ﷺ met them nearby which was a place in the valley of Al Qudayd in the direction of the coast. They were beaten and some were even killed. Women, their offsprings, camels and sheep were all taken as captives.

Translator's note[161]

---

[159] Bukhari (7500/4141)

[160] (31-32/6)

[161] Al Harith Bin Dirar mobilized his men to attack Al Madinah where the Muslims lived. See: The Sealed Nectar p.436 by Sh. Saifur Rahman Mubarakpuri

وَدُومَةُ الْجَنْدَلِ قِبَلَ وَحَصَلْ	عَقْدُ ابْنَةِ الْحَارِثِ بَعْدُ وَاتَّصَلْ

In the area of Jandal before it took place

a contract to Harith's daughter was embraced

وَدُومَةُ الْجَنْدَلِ - A city which was not well-known sitting in the area of modern day 'Al Jawf'.

قِبَلَ – Before the the battle of Banu Mustalliq was the invasion of Dowma Al Jandal (Dumah of the Stone) that took place in Rabee Al Awwal in the 5th year of the hijrah. The invasion of Banee Mastalliq happened in that same year but in the month of Sha'ban as Ibn Al Qaayim[162] established alongside others from the people of knowledge.

وَحَصَلْ – From the results of the battle of Banee Mustalliq.

عَقْدُ – The Messenger of Allah ﷺ married the daughter of Al Haarith named Juwayriya Bint Al Haarith (May Allah be pleased with her), a captive from the tribe of Banee Mustalliq. She was caught by the arrow of Thabit ibn Qays and wrote that she wanted to marry the Prophet ﷺ who then married her and freed one hundred people from her tribe.

بَعْدُ - After the battle of Banu Mustalliq.

[162] (206/3)

وَاتَّصَلْ - That he consummated the marriage with his wife.

وَعَقْدُ رَيْحَانَةَ فِي ذِي الْخَامِسَةْ	ثُمَّ بَنُو لِحْيَانَ بَدْءُ السَّادِسَةْ

Wedded Rayhanah in the fifth of that year

then battled Banu Lihyan in the sixth to occur

وَعَقْدُ رَيْحَانَةَ - He wedded Rayhanah bint Zayd (May Allah be pleased with her) the Prophet's captive from (Banu Quraydha). He freed her and married her and this was one view. Another group mentioned she was from the concubines that the nations before practiced. This was the opinion of Ibn Al Qayyim, Ibn Katheer and others[163] , Al Saalihee describes 'This is the statement of Khalaa'iq[164]

Translator's note[165]

فِي ذِي الْخَامِسَةْ - In the 5th year of the hijrah of Al Islam.

ثُمَّ بَنُو لِحْيَانَ بَدْءُ السَّادِسَة - Occured the battle of Banu Lihyan in the month of Jumad Al Awlaa in the 6th year, the most accurate account. Additionlly this time frame resembled what Al Haafidh ibn Katheer [Rahimullah] mentions in his work '*Al Fusool*'[166]. A battle that caused a

[163] See: Zaad Al Ma'ad (113/1). Al Fusool by Ibn Katheer (238-239)
[164] Subul Al Hudaa wal Rashaad (138/12)
[165] Many previous nations's before practiced this. These concubines had to be cared for and looked after, they were unmarried however if they were impregnated, they were married to and provided for receiving all their rights as wives.
[166] Page 151

group of Muslims to change route to the expedition of Raji and chased the Lihyan tribe to the tops of the mountains for killing ten believers, the Prophet ﷺ then left them and nobody was killed or fought against.

وَبَعْدَه اسْتِسْقَاؤُهُ وَذُو قَرَد[167] وَصُدَّ عَنْ عُمْرَتِهِ لَمَّا قَصَدْ

After it rained and the Dhi Qird mission

they were prevented from their umrah vision

وَبَعْدَه - After this encounter.

اسْتِسْقَاؤُهُ - Ibn Atheer explains 'In this (the 6th year) the people experienced a drought so the messenger of Allah ﷺ prayed and supplicated for rain to descend in which was granted (by Allah).[168] Ibn Al Qayyim [Rahimullah] wrote in *Za'ad Al Ma'ad*[169] 'the Messenger of Allah ﷺ prayed for rain in one of the battles they had with the idol worshippers without mentioning the rain to descend in that specific year.

It was said that he prayed and supplicated in one of the battles until the idol worshippers got to the water first finishing it and left the believers tremendously thirsty so they complained to the Prophet about this problem. The hypocrites said "If you were a true prophet you would pray for rain for your people just like Musaa [Alayhis Salaam] prayed for rain for his". This comment reached the Prophet ﷺ he replied 'or they

[167] Not 'Dhi Waqr' (alternative pronunciation)
[168] Asad Al Ghabah (29/1)
[169] (458/1)

should have asked their Lord to send down upon them rain'. He ﷺ then extended his arms and supplicated to Allah [The Most High] and he did not return his hands except that the clouds surrounded them and it rained profusely. The valley suddenly overfilled and the people began to drink until they were quenched.

Abu Awannah also narrated this from the Sahihah[170] and 'Aishah Bint Sa'd ibn Abi Waqqas narrates from her father (May Allah be pleased with her).

وَذُو قَرَد - The battle of Dhu Qird happened after the event of Banu Lihyan by a few nights. Al Hafidh ibn Katheer records in '*Al Fusool*'[171] 'The attack happened after they entered Al Madinah by a few nights. Uyaynah Bin Husayn at bani Abdullah Bin Ghatfaan saw a small camel of the Prophet ﷺ that bore a lot of milk[172] which he stole in the forest and killed its shepherd. The man was from the Al Ghiffar tribe and he and his bandits also kidnapped the shepherd's wife.

One of the first people who vowed (for revenge) was Salamah ibn Al Akwaa Al Aslamee (May Allah be pleased with him) looking for them on foot. He stumbled across their party trying to escape and was not to be outrun so he shot them with arrows and proclaimed: 'Take that! I am Ibn Al Akwaa, today is the day of revenge!'.

These villians had everything they took retrieved from their hands. When they heard a screeching sound the Prophet ﷺ came out with a group of knights and found Salamah ibn Al Akwaa who had retreieved

[170] No. 2514
[171] Pg. 101-102
[172] The plural form refers to a group of camels that stay in its place possessing a lot of milk.

the stolen camels. The Prophet ﷺ reached a water point that was called Dhu Qard because there was a river for the camels to drink from. He stayed there for one day and one night before returning back to Al Madinah.

وَصُدَّ - The Prophet ﷺ was prevented.

عَنْ عُمْرَتِهِ لَمَّا قَصَدْ - On the journey to Makkah wishing to perform minor pilgrimage (Umrah) he was blockaded. The 6th year of the Hijrah of Al Islam at the battle of Al Hudaybiyah was where the Prophet ﷺ came out with one thousand or so of his companions (May Allah have mercy upon them all), their Umrah was not made easy in their travel. They had to negotiate with the Quraysh upon certain conditions and were not allowed to perform Umrah that year but to return and perform it the following year. The Prophet accepted the conditions and did not make umrah that year. This peace treaty between the Muslims and the mushrikeen acted a great opening as was stated by Ibn Mas'ood and others.[173]

Translator's note[174]

وَبَيْعَةُ الرِّضْوَانِ أُولَى وَبَنَى	فِيهَا بِرَيْحَانَةَ هَذَا بَيِّنَا

The first pledge they built was pleasing and keen

the news of Rayhanah was inbetween

---

[173] See: Al Fusool by Ibn Katheer (159-161)

[174] The peace treaty stipulated that there would be no fighting or bloodshed for at least ten years between the two parties.

وَبَيْعَةُ الرِّضْوَانِ أُولَ - Before the treaty of Hudaybiyah the Prophet ﷺ dispatched Uthman Ibn Affan (May Allah be pleased with him) to Makkah to sort the affair out with the idol worshippers concerning the prevented Umrah however the news travelled back to the Muslims that Uthman had been killed. The Prophet ﷺ then pledged with his glorious companions to fight them, this was named the pledge of Al Ridhwaan which Allah revealed:

﴿لَقَد رَضِيَ اللَّهُ عَنِ المُؤمِنينَ إِذ يُبايِعونَكَ تَحتَ الشَّجَرَةِ فَعَلِمَ

ما في قُلوبِهِم فَأَنزَلَ السَّكينَةَ عَلَيهِم وَأَثابَهُم فَتحًا قَريبًا﴾

{Certainly was Allah pleased with the believers when they pledged allegiance to you, [O Muhammad], under the tree, and He knew what was in their hearts, so He sent down tranquillity upon them and rewarded them with an imminent conquest} (Al Fat'h: 18)

Translators note[175]

وَبَنَى فِيهَا – This year (he built)

بِرَيْحَانَة – Rayhanah Bint Zayd (May Allah be pleased with her) whom we already have mentioned previously. Ibn Al Qayyim [Rahimullah] has

[175] Uthmaan was dispatched to Makkah to inform the Quraysh that the Muslims wanted to perform Umrah and had not come to rage war. He was sent because he had relatives from them (Pagan Makkans) that would not harm him while explaining such. Additionally, he travelled to inform the believers still left in Makkah that there was a conquest soon to happen and Allah's religion will prevail in Makkah. The Quraysh offered Uthman to circumbulate the Ka'bah but he refused doing so without the Prophet ﷺ in which they imprisoned him and news gathered he was killed.

said in his '*Tahqeeq'* that she was a servant of the Prophet ﷺ and not married to him.

هَذَا بَيِّنَا - This was clear regarding this matter.

وَفُرِضَ الْحَجُّ بِخُلْفٍ فَاسْمَعَهْ   وَكَانَ فَتْحُ خَيْبَرٍ فِي السَّابِعَةْ

The Hajj was obligated dispite what was heard

the conquest of Khaybar in the seventh year

وَفُرِضَ الْحَجُّ - In the 6th year the major pilgrimage was mandated (Al Hajj).

بِخُلْفٍ - There was a difference of opinion about this. Al Hafidh ibn Katheer explained in '*Al Fusool*'[176] 'a number of scholars mentioned the Hajj taking place in the 6th year and others have stated in the 9th year; others have also added ten years however this is a very peculiar stance. The strangest view is that presented by the Imam of the Haramayn in his book '*Al Nihayah'* along with some contemporaries that Hajj was obligated before the hijrah.

وَكَانَ فَتْحُ خَيْبَرٍ فِي السَّابِعَة - The conquest of Khaybar began in the 7th year after the hijrah of the Prophet ﷺ. This is the opinion of the majority of scholars and people of knowledge. Ibn Al Qayyim said in 'Zaad Al Ma'ad'[177] 'Musaa Ibn Uqbah said "When the Prophet ﷺ reached

[176] Al Usool of ibn Katheer (Pg 206)
[177] (316/3)

Madinah from Al Hudaybiyah he stayed for twenty days or close to that until he departed to Khaybar in which he engaged in battle there". Allah [The Most High] had promised them victory (battle) in Al Hudaybiyah. Maalik said "the conquest of Khaybar was in the 6th year whilst the the majority stuck to the opinion of the 7th year".

وَحظْرُ لَحْمِ الْحُمُرِ الْأَهْلِيَّةْ   فِيهَا وَمُتْعَةِ النِّسَا الرَّوِيَّةْ

Domesticated donkey's meat not to be consumed

and temporary marriages were refused

وَحظْر - The meat (food) of domesticated donkeys was prohibited.

فِيهَا - In the 7th year of the hijrah.

وَمُتْعَةِ النِّسَا - The temporary marriages (Mutah) with women were also prohibited.

الرَّدِيَّة - The one who carries out this evil action is a corrupt person.

On the day of Al Khaybar events were narrated throughout many of the ahadeeth found in the Sahihayn[178]

On the authority of Ali ibn Abi Taalib (May Allah be pleased with him) 'The Messenger of Allah ﷺ prohibited the consumption of meat of

[178] Bukharee: 5115 / Muslim: 1407

domesticated donkeys and also the temporary contractual marriage agreement with women'.

ثُمَّ عَلَى أُمِّ حَبِيبَةَ عَقَدْ   وَمَهْرَهَا عَنْه[179] النَّجَاشِيُّ نَقَدْ

Then with Umm Habibah he wedded next

with Najashi's help, by the text

ثُمَّ عَلَى أُمِّ حَبِيبَةَ - Ramla Bint Abi Sufyaan (May Allah be pleased with her).

عَقَدْ - He ﷺ wedded her

وَمَهْرَهَا عَنْهُ النَّجَاشِيُّ نَقَدْ - King Negus (of Abysinnia) fixed the price of her dowry for the Prophet ﷺ to pay. We find in '*Zaad Al Ma'ad*'[180] by Ibn Al Qayyim 'He married Umm Habibah, her name was Ramla Bint Abi Sufyan Sakhr bin Harb Al Qurayshee Al Amoweeyah. Some people have said her name was Hind, she was married in the land of Abysinnia as she settled as a migrant there. Najashi stated a dowry of four hundred dinars and it was sent to her from there.

[179] Paid on her behalf
[180] (109/1)

وَسُمَّ فِي شَاةٍ بِهَا هَدِيَّةْ　　　ثُمَّ اصْطَفَى صَفِيَّةً صَفِيَّةْ

The poisonous sheep a gift he received

then he chose Safiyyah for her manners and deeds

وَسُمَّ - An attempt to poison to the Prophet ﷺ.

فِي شَاة - Poision was placed inside this cooked sheep.

بِهَا - In the 7th year of the hijrah when they conquered Khaybar.

هَدِيَّة - It was meant to be a gift for the Prophet ﷺ from a Jewish woman. An account of this is mentioned in the Sahihayn[181] from the hadith of Anas ibn Malik (May Allah be pleased with him) and others.

ثُمَّ اصْطَفَى - The Prophet chose صَفِيَّةْ Safiyyah Bint Huyay (May Allah be pleased with her).

صَفِيَّةْ - She was a captive from Al Khaybar and embraced Islam. The Prophet freed her and married her which was reported by Anas Ibn Malik from Al Bukharee and Muslim.[182]

---

[181] Bukharee 2617 / Muslim 2190
[182] Bukharee 271 / Muslim 1365

ثُمَّ أَتَتْ وَمَنْ بَقِي مُهَاجِرَا وَعَقْدُ مَيْمُونَةَ كَانَ الآخِرَا

The rest arrived who migrated alas

and then married Maymunah who was the last

ثُمَّ أَتَتْ - Umm Habibah (arrived).

وَ - Along with them was company.

مَنْ بَقِي مُهَاجِرَا – The rest that were in Abysinnia finally arrived such as Ja'far Ibn Abi Talib and others. The Prophet ﷺ said concerning Ja'far's arrival "*I don't know which makes me happier, the arrival of Ja'far or the conquering of Khaybar*".[183]

وَعَقْدُ مَيْمُونَة – Bint Al Harith Al Halaaleyah (May Allah be pleased with her)

كَانَ الآخِرَ – The Prophet ﷺ married no other woman after Maymoonah.

Ibn Al Qayyim [Rahimullah] explains 'He then married Maymoonah Bint Al Harith Al Halaaleeyah who was the last woman he wedded. They were married in Makkah after the make-up Umrah and she was made lawful for him.

[183] Reported by Tabarani in 'Al Mu'jim Al Kabeer' 100/22 no.244. Al Albanee also mentions it in 'Al Silsilah As-Saheehah'

وَقَبْلُ إِسْلاَمُ أَبِي هُرَيْرَةْ وَبَعْدُ عُمْرَةُ الْقَضَا الشَّهِيرَةْ

But before was the Islam of Abu Hurayrah

after was the famous Umrah saviour

وَقَبْلُ - Prior to this.

إِسْلاَمُ أَبِي هُرَيْرَةَ - The acceptance of Islam by Abu Hurayrah (May Allah be pleased with him) was slightly before the event of Al Khaybar. He approached the Prophet ﷺ at Al Khaybar but didn't take part in the battle.[184]

وَبَعْدُ - After the battle of Al Khaybar it was the famous make-up Umrah (Umratul Qadhaa). When he ﷺ returned back to Al Madinah from Al Khaybar he stayed until the month of Dhil Qi'dah. He then left to perform Umrah **عُمْرَةُ الْقَضَا الشَّهِيرَة** due to the Quraysh preventing him the previous year. He ﷺ continued until he reached Makkah and circumbulated the Sacred House to complete the rituals of Umrah.[185]

[184] See: Sahih Al Bukharee 2827

[185] See: Seerah Ibn Hishaam (1199-1197/2)

وَالرُّسْلَ فِي مُحَرَّمِ الْمُحَرَّمِ[186] أَرْسَلَهُمْ إِلَى الْمُلُوكِ فَاعْلَمِ

The messengers next in Muharram brought

Islamic letters to the kings they were taught

وَالرُّسْل - The blessed companions of the Messenger of Allah ﷺ acted as messengers (that were sent out) .

فِي مُحَرَّمِ الْمُحَرَّمِ - In the blessed month of Allah Muharram amongst the four sacred months.

أَرْسَلَهُمْ - The Prophet ﷺ dispatched some of his companions when they returned from Al Hudaybiah.

إِلَى الْمُلُوكِ فَاعْلَمِ - He sent a number of companions out, each one carried a letter for a king whom they were sent to. Umar Ibn Umayyah Al Dhameeri was sent to Negus, the king of Abysinnia. Daheeya Al Kalby travelled to Ceasar, the king of Rome. Abdullah Ibn Hudhayfah Al Sahmee to Kisraa, the king of Persia and Haatib ibn Abi Balt'ah to Al Muqawqis, the ruler of Egypt. Other companions were also sent on similar delegations (May Allah be pleased with all of them).[187]

On the authority of Anas ibn Malik (May Allah be pleased with him) narrates the Prophet ﷺ had a letter written for Kisraa, Najashi and every

[186] Haram (Makkah)
[187] See: Zaad Al Ma'ad (119-124/1)

powerful mighty ruler calling them to the humble message to worship Allah [The Most High].[188]

وَأُهْدِيَتْ مَارِيَةُ الْقِبْطِيَّةْ فِيهِ وَفِي الثَّامِنَةِ السَّرِيَّةْ

Mariah the Coptic was truly a gift stated

in the eighth year delegated

لِمُؤْتَةٍ سَارَتْ وَفِي الصِّيَامِ قَدْ كَانَ فَتْحُ الْبَلَدِ الْحَرَامِ

Mu'tah begun during the fast

then the conquest of the Haram finally passed

وَأُهْدِيَتْ مَارِيَةُ الْقِبْطِيَّةْ - Al Muqawqis, the ruler of Askandria presented her (Mariah the Coptic) to the Prophet ﷺ as a gift.

فِيه - In the month of Muharram in the 7th year after the hijrah a letter was returned back to the Prophet ﷺ replying with "May it have goodness for all" but he did not accept Al Islam instead he gifted the Prophet ﷺ a slave maiden named Mariah the Coptic.

وَفِي الثَّامِنَةِ - In the 8th year of the Islamic calendar.

[188] Muslim (1774)

لِمُؤْتَةٍ سَارَتْ - Ibn Katheer [Rahimullah] states 'In the month of Jumaad Al Aakhir in the 8th year summoned the call of Al Mu'tah which is a village in the land of Al Shaam.'[189] The Prophet ﷺ informed his companions what happened (during a sermon) with regards to the group of heroes there as reported in Sahih Al Bukharee[190]

Narrated Anas bin Malik:

The Prophet ﷺ said "Zaid took over the flag and was martyred. Then it was taken by Jafar who was martyred as well. Then 'Abdullah bin Rawaha took the flag but he too was martyred" and at that time the eyes of Allah's Apostle were full of tears. "Then Khalid bin Al-Walid took the flag without being nominated as a chief (beforehand) and was blessed with victory."

وَفِي - That month

الصِّيَامِ - The 8th year after the major hijrah to Al Madinah[191]

قَدْ كَانَ فَتْحُ الْبَلَدِ الْحَرَام - This conquest (of the sacred land Makkah) was mentioned by Allah in the Quran by his words :

﴿لاَ يَسْتَوِي مِنْكُمْ مَنْ أَنْفَقَ مِنْ قَبْلِ الْفَتْحِ وَقَاتَلَ أُوْلَئِكَ أَعْظَمُ دَرَجَةً مِنْ الَّذِينَ أَنْفَقُوا مِنْ بَعْدُ وَقَاتَلُوا﴾

---

[189] Al Fusool fi seeratil Rusool (Pg. 170)
[190] No. 3063
[191] See: Seerah Ibn Hishaam (1229/2)

{Not equal among you are those who spent before the conquest [of Makkah] and fought [and those who did so after it]. Those are greater in degree than they who spent afterwards and fought} (Al Hadid: 10)

وَبَعْدَهُ قَدْ أَوْرَدُوا مَا كَانَ فِي	يَوْمِ حُنَيْنٍ ثُمَّ يَوْمِ الطَّائِفِ

Next it was relayed about the day

prior toTaif it was Hunayn

وَبَعْدَهُ - After the conquest of Makkah in the 8th year.

قَدْ أَوْرَدُوا - Collected and compiled by the scholars of the seerah and the battles of Islam.[192]

مَا كَانَ فِي يَوْمِ حُنَيْنٍ - That day was also named the battle of Awtaas. It is a place between Makkah and Taif hence it was given the title of its place. Another name given was 'The battle of Hawazan' because of those from the Hawazan tribe that fought alongside the Prophet ﷺ.[193]

ثُمَّ يَوْمِ الطَّائِفِ - The battle of Taif occured in the month of Shawaal in the 8th year of the hijrah. Before he returned from Hunayn he ﷺ did not

[192] See: Seerah Ibn Hisham (1283/2)
[193] Zaad Al Ma'ad - Ibn Qayyim (465/3)

enter Makkah except that he continued on to Taif to battle and was prevented and returned without fighting.[194]

وَبَعْدُ[195] فِي ذِي الْقَعْدَةِ اعْتِمَارُهْ مِنَ الْجِعِرَّانَةِ وَاسْتِقْرَارُهْ

After Dhil Qi'dah his Umrah he started

Ja'irranah to Makkah the Prophet departed

وَبَعْدُ - The month of Dhil' Qiddah

اعْتِمَارُهْ - The Prophet ﷺ was going to perform his Umrah.

مِنَ الْجِعِرَّانَةِ - A place between Makkah and Taif but it is closer to Makkah.

وَاسْتِقْرَارُه - He stayed in Ji'ranah for ten nights[196] then performed Umrah.

After his Umrah was completed he returned back to Al Madinah. There then he left Attab ibn Aseed[197] as the leader over the people there even though he was under twenty years of age.[198]

---

[194] See: Seerah Ibn Hishaam (1330/2)
[195] After
[196] See: Sahih Al Bukharee no.4319
[197] Seerah Ibn Hishaam (1352-1353/2)
[198] See: Zaad Al Ma'ad (126/1)

وَبِنْتُهُ زَيْنَبُ مَاتَتْ ثُمَّا   مَوْلِدُ إِبْرَاهِيمَ فِيهَا حَتْمَا

His daughter Zaynab passed after some time

Ibrahim was born after she died

وَبِنْتُهُ زَيْنَبُ مَاتَتْ - Zaynab the daughter of the Prophet ﷺ passed away.

ثُمَّا - A nice word acting as a connective which can also refer to months later.

مَوْلِدُ إِبْرَاهِيم - The birth of the Prophet's son ﷺ Ibraheem.

فِيهَا - The 8th year of the prophetic hijrah.

حَتْم - With certainty he passed away in the early stages of his birth.

وَوَهَبَتْ نَوْبَتَهَا لِعَائِشَةْ   سَوْدَةُ مَا دَامَتْ زَمَانًا عَائِشَةْ

She donated to Aishah a great sacrifice

Sawdah with goodness a wonderful wife

It was the mother of the believers Sawdah (May Allah be pleased with her) who sacrificed her day and night with the Prophet ﷺ to Aishah (May Allah be pleased with her). This pleased the Prophet greatly and she remained with him. This beautiful effort was also transmitted by Imam Tirmidhee in his work *'Al Jamiah'*[199].

On the authority of Ibn Abbas (May Allah be pleased with him) he said:

"*Sawdah feared that the Messenger of Allah might divorce her and she said "O Messenger of Allah! Do not divorce me, give my day to A'ishah which he did. Later, Allah revealed unto him:*

﴿وَإِنِ امْرَأَةٌ خَافَتْ مِنْ بَعْلِهَا نُشُوزًا أَوْ إِعْرَاضًا فَلَا جُنَاحَ عَلَيْهِمَا﴾

{And if a woman fears cruelty or desertion on her husband's part, there is no sin on them both.} (Al Nisaa: 128)

Ibn Abbas said, "Whatever (legal agreement) the spouses mutually agree to is allowed."

وَعُمِلَ الْمِنْبَرُ غَيْرَ مُخْتَفِ   وَحَجَّ عَتَّابٌ بِأَهْلِ الْمَوْقِفِ

A pulpit was made clear to see

then the Hajj of Attab led the city

وَعُمِلَ الْمِنْبَرَ – A pulpit was constructed for him ﷺ to deliver sermons to the believers.

غَيْرَ مُخْتَفِ – A place which was not hidden being a place in the masjid.

Ibn Al Atheer wrote 'In the 8th year a pulpit (minbar) was built for him ﷺ

[199] No. 3040. Tirmidhee said that the hadith is Hassan ghareeb. It has also been graded Hassan by Ibn Hajr in 'Al Isaabah' (1506/13)

to deliver sermon ﷺ and used to lecture on its trunk. Once the trunk of wood started to wail until the people heard the sound coming from it, the Messenger of Allah descended the pulpit and placed his hand on the trunk and calmed it, this was the first ever pulpit in Al Islam.[200]

There is a narration from Sahih Bukharee[201] On the authority of Jabir ibn Abdullah (May Allah be pleased with him) said:

A woman asked "*O Allah's Apostle! Shall I get something constructed for you to sit on as I have a slave who is a carpenter?*" He replied, "*Yes, if you like.*" So she had that pulpit constructed. On Friday he used to lean on the minbar that was made for him in which the palm tree (he used to lean on) for Jumuah and it cried profusely. The Prophet ﷺ descended the minbar and started to hold and stroke this tree until it quietened down and said "Indeed it is crying as it used to remember this thikr".

وَحَجَّ عَتَّابٌ - Attab Ibn Usayd (May Allah be pleased with him).

In his book '*Al Isaabah*'[202] Ibn Hajr describes 'He accepted Islam on the day of the conquest. The Prophet ﷺ used the palm trunk on the way to Makkah until he reached Hunayn and continued. It was said 'however it was used upon returning from Taif and he (Attab) led the people for Hajj in the year of the conquest'.

بِأَهْلِ الْمَوْقِفِ - Ibn Katheer says this was the first Hajj that the Muslims followed a leader amongst them (Attab).[203]

---

[200] Asad Al Ghaabah (30/1) See: Tareekh Al Islam by Adh Dhahabi (Maghazi 621)
[201] No. 2095
[202] (62/7)
[203] Al Fusool fi seeratil Rasool (Pg.189)

ثُمَّ تبُوكَ قَدْ غزَا فِي التَّاسِعَةْ وَهَدَّ مَسْجِدَ الضِّرَارِ رَافِعَه[204]

Tabuk a battle in the ninth taking place

destroying Masjid Al Dhiraar after its raise

ثُمَّ تَبُوكَ قَدْ غَزَا فِي التَّاسِعَةْ - The Prophet ﷺ partook in the battle of Tabuk that occurred in the 9th year of the hijrah. Al Hafidh ibn Katheer explained in '*Al Fusool*' Allah sent the verses to His Messenger:

﴿قَاتِلُوا الَّذِينَ لاَ يُؤْمِنُونَ بِاللَّهِ وَلاَ بِالْيَوْمِ الآخِرِ وَلاَ يُحَرِّمُونَ مَا حَرَّمَ اللَّهُ وَرَسُولُهُ وَلاَ يَدِينُونَ دِينَ الْحَقِّ مِنَ الَّذِينَ أُوتُوا الْكِتَابَ حَتَّى يُعْطُوا الْجِزْيَةَ عَنْ يَدٍ وَهُمْ صَاغِرُونَ﴾

{Fight those who do not believe in Allah or in the Last Day and who do not consider unlawful what Allah and His Messenger have made unlawful and who do not adopt the religion of truth from those who were given the Scripture - [fight] until they give the jizyah willingly while they are humbled.} (Al Tawbah: 29)

He ﷺ dispatched a group of the Madinans and those around them from the Arabian tribes to partake in the various battles to defend Al Islam. He ﷺ also informed them about the battle of Rome in the month of Rajab in the 9th year. He called them to be prepared for the harsh conditions of warfare. They could not grow fruits as it was a dry and infertile year which they were prepared for anyway. When the Muslims

[204] An event that occurred.

reached their destination they did not partake in the battle because upon entering the land of Shaam they did not find them. That year they split from them and he called for their return.

وَهَدَّ - The Prophet ﷺ demolished.

مَسْجِدَ الضِّرَار - A mosque of opposition was tore down on the journey back from Tabuk.

رَافِعَه - Then raised the mosque that was purposely built for him.

Translators note[205]

وَحَجَّ بِالنَّاسِ أَبُو بَكْرٍ وَثَمّْ   تَلا بَرَاءَةً عَلِيٌّ وَحَتَم

Abu Bakr lead on the Hajj occasion

then Ali declared the emancipation

[205] Masjid Al Dhirar was built by the men of Abu Amir, a Christian monk. He and his menwere hyprocrites disguised as Muslims in Madinah. They built a masjid next to Masjid Al Qubaa and concealed weapons and armor in it to attack the Prophet ﷺ. To make it more believable they requested the Prophet ﷺ to pray in it so the Muslims would understand it as an approval. When the revelation came about their evil schemes the Prophet ordered for it to be destroyed upon his return from Tabuk.

أَنْ لَا يَحُجَّ مُشْرِكٌ بَعْدُ وَلاَ يَطُوفُ عَارٍ ذَا بِأَمْرٍ فُعِلاَ

No pagans will perform Hajj on their standard

or make the Tawaaf other than commanded

وَحَجَّ بِالنَّاسِ أَبُو بَكْرٍ - In the 9th year of the hijrah Abu Bakr As Sidiq (May Allah be pleased with him) led the people in the pilgrimage of Hajj.

وَثَمَّ تَلا بَرَاءَةً عَلِيٌّ - Here Ali (May Allah be pleased with him) emancipates from the people of idol worship. Allah revealed:

﴿بَرَاءَةٌ مِنَ اللَّهِ وَرَسُولِهِ إِلَى الَّذِينَ عَاهَدْتُمْ مِنَ الْمُشْرِكِينَ﴾

{This is a declaration of] disassociation, from Allah and His Messenger, to those with whom you had made a treaty among the polytheists}
(Al Tawbah: 1)

وَحَتَم - A matter was made clear and decided.

أَنْ لَا يَحُجَّ مُشْرِكٌ بَعْدُ وَلاَ يَطُوفُ عَارٍ - The pagan arabs used to hold onto their old rituals of their pilgrimage (that which opposed Islam and its monotheistic practices). It was mentioned in the Sahihayn[206] On the narration of Abu Hurayrah (May Allah be pleased with him), he said:

[206] Bukharee 4655 / Muslim 1347

"During that Hajj (in which Abu Bakr was the chief of the pilgrims) Abu Bakr sent me along with announcers on the Day of Nahr (10th of Dhul-Hijja) in Mina to announce "No pagans shall perform Hajj after this year, and none shall perform the Tawaf around the Kabah in a naked state." Humaid bin Abdur Rahman added 'then Allah's Messenger ﷺ sent Ali bin Abi Talib (after Abu Bakr) and ordered him to recite aloud in public Surat Bara'a. Abu Huraira added "So Ali, along with us recited Bara'a (loudly) before the people at Mina on the Day of Nahr and announced "No pagan shall perform Hajj after this year and none shall perform the Tawaf around the Kabah in a naked state."

ذَا بِأَمْرٍ فُعِلاَ - Abu Bakr and Ali fulfilled this command that was ordered by the Prophet ﷺ .

وَجَاءَتِ الْوُفُودُ فِيهَا تَتْرَى	هَذَا وَمِنْ نِسَاهُ آلَى شَهْرَا

The delegations then came in succession

30 days from his wives to teach them a lesson

وَجَاءَتِ الْوُفُودُ فِيهَا - The 9th year of the hijrah was known as 'The Year of the Delegations' due to the increasing amount of groups coming to the Prophet ﷺ.

تَتْرَى – It was delegation after delegation approaching him. Ibn Katheer said 'There were many delegations that year aproaching the Prophet ﷺ

who was keeping firm to the obedience of Allah and thus resulting in many people accepting Islam in large crowds'[207].

هَذَا وَمِنْ نِسَاهُ آلَى شَهْرٍ - As reported in the Sahihayn[208] "The Prophet ﷺ vowed to keep aloof from his wives for a month. After the completion of 29 days he went back either in the morning or in the afternoon to his wives. Someone said to him "You vowed that you would not go to your wives for one month." He replied, "The month is of 29 days."

نِسَاهُ آلَى شَهْرٍ - He vowed that he would not go to his wives for a complete month.

Translators note[209]

ثُمَّ النَّجَاشِيَّ نَعَى وَصَلَّى عَلَيْهِ مِنْ طَيْبَةَ نَالَ[210] الْفَضْلَا
Next passed Najashi they grieved and they prayed
upon this good person the virtue was paid

[207] Al Fusool: 196

[208] Bukharee 1910 / Muslim 1085 from the hadith of Umm Salamah

[209] He vowed that he would keep away from his wives for a month in order to show them that the worldly life was unimportant to him, to teach them a lesson for disclosing his secrets, reduce the jealousy among them and to measure their love of and loyalty to him ﷺ.

[210] Said

ثُمَّ النَّجَاشِيَّ - King Negus of Abyssinia next died whom the companions migrated to escaping the pursection of Makkah. Najashi protected, shielded and hosted them generously under his rulership.

نَعَى - The Prophet ﷺ mourned his death and informed the companions of his passing.

وَصَلَّى عَلَيْهِ - His funeral prayer was performed in Madinah whilst his body was buried in Abyssinia.

مِنْ طَيْبَةَ نَالَ الْفَضْلَا - It was a great virtue upon him that the Prophet ﷺ led the companions from Al Madinah to pray and supplicate for him. It is recorded in the ahadeeth of Bukharee and Muslim[211].

The Prophet ﷺ grieved the death of Najashi on the day he passed away then went out into a prayer place and assembled the lines of the companions and made four takbeeraat (for the prayer).

وَمَاتَ إِبْرَاهِيمُ فِي الْعَامِ الْأَخِيرْ وَالْبَجَلِيْ أَسْلَمَ وَاسْمُهُ جَرِيرْ

In the last year Ibraheem's passing then came

Bajali converted and Jareer was his name

وَمَاتَ إِبْرَاهِيمُ فِي الْعَامِ الْأَخِير - The death of his son occurred in the 10th year of the hijrah. Ibn Hajr describes in 'Al Isaabah'[212] 'He was

[211] Bukharee 1245 / Muslim 951
[212] (337/1) -0500940189

Ibraheem ibn Muhammad ibn Abdullah ibn Abdul Mutallib ibn Hishaam, the prince of mankind whose mother was Maria the Coptic and born in the month of Dhi Hijjah in the 8th year and died in the 10th year'.

وَالْبَجَلِيْ - A sukoon on the 'Yaa' in regards to its pronounciation

أَسْلَمَ وَاسْمُهُ جَرِير - Ibn Abdullah Al Bajalee the great companion accepted Islam this year. Al Waqidy held that he went on a delegation with the Prophet ﷺ in the month of Ramadan in the 10th year, the Prophet ﷺ also sent him to Dhil Khilaysah. [213]

وَحَجَّ حِجَّةَ الْوَدَاعِ قَارِنَا وَوَقَفَ الْجُمْعَةَ فِيهَا آمِنَا

Then performed Hajj, the farewell achieved

they stood on the Friday with convicted belief

وَحَجّ - The Prophet ﷺ performed his Hajj in this year, the last (the 10th) of the hijrah.

حِجَّةَ الْوَدَاعِ - The only Hajj the Prophet ﷺ ever performed was named 'The Farewell Hajj' because he said to his companions "*I do not know if I would be able to perform another Hajj after this one of mine*".[214]

[213] Al Raji As-Saabiq (190-191/2)

[214] Collected by Muslim (1297) from the hadith of Jabir ibn Abdullah (RadhiyAllahu Anh)

قَارِنًا - The most accurate observations amongst the statements of the people of knowledge concerning his pilgrimage is that he ﷺ performed Hajj Al Qiraan with the same Ihram of performing Umrah prior. He also brought his own sacrificial animal with him ﷺ.

Ibn Al Qayyim [Rahimullah] stated in 'Al Zaad'[215] 'There are around twenty authentic narrations that the Prophet ﷺ performed Hajj Al Qiran between them are some which have errors.'

وَوَقَفَ الْجُمْعَةَ فِيهَا آمِنَ - Where they stopped (on Arafah) landed on a Friday. It appears in the Sahihayn[216] on the authority of Umar ibn Al Khattab (May Allah be pleased with him):

That a Jewish man said to him: "*O Commander of the Faithful! There is a verse in your Scripture, if it was revealed to us Jews we would have taken it as a holiday."* Umar asked "*Which verse?*" The man said, ﴿**This day I have perfected your religion for you, completed my favor unto you, and I am pleased to have Islam as your religion**﴾ **(5:3)**" Umar said, "*I know the day and place this [verse] was revealed. It was revealed as the Messenger of Allah, peace upon him, was standing on the Mount of Arafa on the Day of Jumu'ah*".

---

215 (107-122/2)

وَأُنْزِلَتْ فِي الْيَوْمِ بُشْرَى لَكُمُ   اَلْيَوْمَ أَكْمَلْتُ لَكُمْ دِينَكُمْ

The news was revealed on that glorious day

the religion has completed nothing taken away

On this perfect day of Arafah, the maginificent verse was revealed:

﴿الْيَوْمَ أَكْمَلْتُ لَكُمْ دِينَكُمْ وَأَتْمَمْتُ عَلَيْكُمْ نِعْمَتِي وَرَضِيتُ لَكُمُ الْإِسْلَامَ دِينًا﴾

{This day I have perfected your religion for you, completed my favor unto you, and I am pleased to have Islam as your religion} (Al Maidah:3)

We have mentioned the narration with the incident of Umar Al Khattab (May Allah be pleased with him) in the Sahihayn regarding the reminder of 'Glad tidings to you' was given. This was great news for mankind that day that Allah perfected His religion in which we need no other religion except it and no other prophet from His other prophets' ﷺ.

وَمَوْتُ رَيْحَانَةَ بَعْدَ عَوْدِهْ   وَالتِّسْعُ عِشْنَ مُدَّةً مِنْ بَعْدِهْ

Rayhanah died after he returned at last

but the nine remained when he did pass

وَمَوْتُ رَيْحَانَةَ - May Allah be pleased with her

بَعْدَ عَوْدِهْ - A great loss after the Prophet ﷺ returned from Hajj. We started the discussion explaining that Rayhanah was a maiden slave that Allah made permissible for the Prophet ﷺ from Banu Quraydhah, she was a concubine of his and not from his wives ﷺ. Al Haafidh ibn Hajr says in '*Al Isaabah*'[217] 'She passed away sixteen months before the death of the Messenger ﷺ and it is said she died when he returned from the farewell pilgrimage', the latter was also the opinion of the author [Rahimullah].

وَالتِّسْعُ - The nine wives of the Prophet ﷺ

عِشْنَ مُدَّةً مِنْ بَعْدِه - Ibn Al Qayyim said in '*Zaad Al Ma'ad*'[218] 'There is no dispute that the Prophet ﷺ died having nine wives remaining but they were counted as eight due to Sawdah passing away while he was alive, she gave her night away to Aishah (May Allah be pleased with all of them)

وَيَوْمَ الاِثْنَيْنِ قَضَى يَقِينَا إِذْ أَكْمَلَ الثَّلَاثَ وَالسِّتِّينَا

Monday it was the judgment agreed

the completion of his life at sixty three

[217] (402-403/13)
[218] (114/1)

وَالدَّفْنُ فِي بَيْتِ ابْنَةِ الصِّدِّيقِ   فِي مَوْضِعِ الْوَفَاةِ عَنْ تَحْقِيقِ

Buried in her house, daughter of one who bore truth

a place not denied was evidently proof

وَمُدَّةُ التَّمْرِيضِ خُمْسَا شَهْرِ   وَقِيلَ بَلْ ثُلْثٌ[219] وَخُمْسٌ فَاذْرِ

Strucken with illness for a fifth of 30 nights

yet some say a third but a fifth is whats right.

وَيَوْمَ الاِثْنَيْنِ قَضَى - The Prophet ﷺ departed this world on a Monday.

يَقِينًا - The day that he was born, the day he was sent as a Messenger and the day he passed away. It was this day (reported by the two shaykhs)[220] that he captured and slaughtered an animal in the month of Rabee Al Awwal.

On the authority of Anas ibn Maalik (May Allah be pleased with him):

While Abu Bakr was leading the people in the Morning Prayer on a Monday, the Prophet came towards them suddenly having lifted the curtain of Aishah's house and looked at them as they were standing in rows and smiled. Abu Bakr tried to get back into the row thinking that Allah's Apostle wanted to come out for the prayer. The attention of the Muslims was diverted from the prayer because they were delighted to see the Prophet. The Prophet waved his hand to them to complete their

[219] Three

[220] Bukharee 4448 / Muslim 419 with his wording

prayer then he went back into the room and let down the curtain. The Prophet departed on that very day.

إِذْ أَكْمَلَ الثَّلَاثَ وَالسِّتِّينَا - His passing away at the age sixty three. It is recorded in the Sahihayn[221] on the authority of Aishah (May Allah be pleased with her) that the Prophet ﷺ passed away when he was sixty-three years of age.

On the authority of Anas ibn Malik (May Allah be pleased with him) the Prophet passed away at sixty-three, Abu Bakr also passed away at sixty-three and Umar also died at sixty-three. This is found in the hadith of Imam Muslim[222]

وَالدَّفْنُ فِي بَيْتِ ابْنَةِ الصِّدِّيقِ - He ﷺ was buried in the house of Aishah in her private chamber (of the masjid).

Translators note[223].

فِي مَوْضِعِ الْوَفَاةِ - He was buried in his place due to the saying of his "*No prophet is buried anywhere except the place that he passes away.*"[224] He was buried according to the correct Islamic procedure whereby his rights were fulfilled, hence the author words عَنْ تَحْقِيقِ.

[221] Bukharee 3036-4422 / Muslim 2349
[222] Muslim 2348
[223] Aishah's home was attached to the masjid and was still within the confinds of the masjid of the Prophet ﷺ
[224] Recorded by Imam Ahmad in his Musnad (27) from the hadith of Abu Bakr Al Sideeq (May Allah be pleased with him. Also Sahih Al Jaami' (5201)

Also the hadith in the Sahihayn[225] on the report of Aishah (May Allah be pleased with her) she said the Prophet ﷺ was asking repeatedly during his illness "*Where am I today? Where will I be tomorrow?" and I was waiting for my day (impatiently). Then, when my turn came (being with him), Allah took his soul away (in my lap) between my chest and arms and he was buried in my house*".

Imam Al Tirmidhee reported this in '*Ash Shamaa'il*' and Imam Al Nasaa'i in *As-Sunnan Al Kubraa*'[226] which has an authentic chain from Saalim ibn Ubayd who was amongst the companions known as 'Suffah'.

They said the Prophet ﷺ fainted while he was sick and then woke up. It is a long hadith which the people said to Abu Bakr "*O companion of the Messenger of Allah ﷺ did you bury the Messenger of Allah ﷺ?*" which he replied "*Yes*" they asked "*Where?*" and he replied "*In the place that Allah took his soul away and He [The Most High] did not take his soul except in a good place, know that He has been truthful*".

وَمُدَّةُ التَّمْرِيضِ - He ﷺ was ill for a fixed amount of time until he departed this world.

خُمْسَا شَهْرِ - The time frame is said to be a fifth of the month: six days , i.e two fifths as twelve days, this is one stance.

(وَقِيلَ بَلْ ثُلْثٌ) - Another view is a third of a month which equates to ten days

[225] Bukharee 1389/ Muslim 2443
[226] Shamaa'il (397) Sunnan Al Kubraa (7119)

وَخُمْسٌ - But a fifth of the month e.g six days when added to ten days totals sixteen days. It seems the position of six days is the closest.

Ibn Katheer explains in '*Al Fusool*'[227] research shows that it was twelve days and others state fourteen days. Al Hafidh ibn Hajr says in '*Fat'h Al Baaree*'[228] 'there is a difference regarding the duration of his sickness but the majority hold that it was thirteen days and others increased by a day while others went lower, it has been mentioned as ten days also'.

فَادْر - You should stress on the letter yaa.

وَتَمَّتِ الْأُرْجُوزَةُ الْمِيئِيَّةْ   فِي ذِكْرِ حَالِ أَشْرَفِ الْبَرِيَّةْ

We complete this poem of one hundred lines

on the best of creation that was ever alive

صَلَّى عَلَيْهِ اللهُ رَبِّي وَعَلَى   صِحَابِهِ وآلِهِ وَمَنْ تَلا

Prayers be upon him and also upon

his companions and family that continued on

وَتَمَّتِ الْأُرْجُوزَةُ الْمِيئِيَّةْ - The total number of couplets have reached one hundred as was named 'Al Arjooz Al Mee'iyah' (One Hundred Lines of Poetry).

[227] (201)
[228] (129/8)

فِي ذِكْرِ حَالِ أَشْرَفِ الْبَرِيَّة - The most noble of creation is the Messenger of Allah ﷺ. This piece of poetry is an exquisite summary of certain selected events from the biography of the Messenger of Allah ﷺ. Its narrative is explained briefly with reference to the history and dates.

صَلَّى عَلَيْهِ اللهُ رَبِّي - A conclusion to this brilliantly written and highly beneficial poem that prays and praises our beloved Prophet ﷺ.

وَعَلَى صِحَابِهِ وآلِهِ - The blessed companions that surrounded the Prophet ﷺ male and female.

وَمَنْ تَلا - Those who followed him ﷺ in his footsteps of righteousness until the day of reckoning.

I ask Allah the most generous, the master of his throne to bestow the author Al Imam ibn Abi Al Ezz Al Hanafee [Rahimullah] the best reward for this eloquent work of poetry and allow this to be weighed with his good deeds on the day we meet Allah. I also ask Allah to raise his ranks, to benefit us all in what we have learned, make this a proof for us and not against us and finally to guide us to the straight path.

O Allah, we ask You for continuous faith and beneficial knowledge to be guided aright[229]. The ability is for You of whom You love and are pleased with from the concise statements we make and the pious actions and

[229] A report for this dua comes from Ibn Abi Shaybah in (Al Emaan) no.107/ Narrated Mu'awiyah ibn Quraat who said: Abu Dardaa said: Muawiyah mentioned: We see from faith is faith which is not always present, and from knowledge is knowledge that doesn't always benefit, and from guidance is guidance may not always lead you to the right path. Allahu Al Musta'aan.

Allah knows best. We finally send the peace and blessings upon our Prophet and Messenger Muhammad ﷺ, his family and his companions (May Allah be pleased with all of them). Ameen.

سُبْحَانَكَ اللَّهُمَّ وَبِحَمْدِكَ أَشْهَدُ أَنْ لا إِلَهَ إِلا أَنْتَ
أَسْتَغْفِرُكَ وَأَتُوبُ إِلَيْكَ

<u>For Translation Work:</u>

hijaaztranslate@gmail.com

YouTube Channel: Hijaaz Translate

Printed in the United States
By Bookmasters